Mastering Legal Tech And AI

Tools, Trends, Innovations, and Transformations That Lawyers, Law Students and Professional Must Know in Modern Law Practice and Justice.

-- By Louis Coleman --

Text Copyright © by Louis Coleman

All rights reserved. No part of this guide may be reproduced in any form without permission in writing from the publisher except in the case of brief quotations embodied in critical articles or reviews.

Legal & Disclaimer

The information contained in this book and its contents is not designed to replace or take the place of any form of medical or professional advice; and is not meant to replace the need for independent medical, financial, legal or other professional advice or services, as may be required. The content and information in this book have been provided for educational and entertainment purposes only.

The content and information contained in this book have been compiled from sources deemed reliable, and it is accurate to the best of the Author's knowledge, information, and belief. However, the Author cannot guarantee its accuracy and validity and cannot be held liable for any errors and/or omissions. Further, changes are periodically made to this book as and when needed. Where appropriate and/or necessary, you must consult a professional (including but not limited to your doctor, attorney, financial advisor or such other professional advisor) before using any of the suggested remedies, techniques, or information in this book.

Upon using the contents and information contained in this book, you agree to hold harmless the Author from and against any damages, costs, and expenses, including any legal fees potentially resulting from the application of any of the information provided by this book. This disclaimer applies to any loss, damages or injury caused by the use and application, whether directly or indirectly, of any advice or information presented, whether for breach of contract, tort, negligence, personal injury, criminal intent, or under any other cause of action.

You agree to accept all risks of using the information presented inside this book.

You agree that by continuing to read this book, where appropriate and/or necessary, you shall consult a professional (including but not limited to your doctor, attorney, or financial advisor or such other advisor as needed) before using any of the suggested remedies, techniques, or information in this book.

TABLE OF CONTENTS

INTRODUCTION 6
LEGAL TECH INTRODUCTION: WHY IT MATTERS AND HOW IT'S CHANGING LAW 8
LEGAL TECH ADOPTION TODAY: TRENDS, INSIGHTS, AND FUTURE FORECASTS 12
EXPLORE THE HISTORY OF LEGAL TECH: KEY MILESTONES AND TECHNOLOGIES THAT HAVE DEFINED ITS DEVELOPMENT 16
UNDERSTANDING THE VARIOUS ASPECTS OF THE LEGAL TECH LANDSCAPE 20
LEGAL SERVICE DELIVERY: EXPLORE DIVERSE APPROACHES AND BENEFITS 24
PRACTICAL APPLICATIONS OF LEGAL TECH: HOW TECHNOLOGY IS SHAPING LEGAL PRACTICE 29
E-DISCOVERY ESSENTIALS: KEY COMPONENTS AND PRACTICAL INSIGHTS 34
LEGAL RESEARCH AND ANALYTICS: ESSENTIAL TOOLS AND TECHNIQUES 40
BOOSTING EFFICIENCY IN LAW: LEVERAGING TECHNOLOGY FOR BETTER RESULTS 45
MASTERING CONTRACT MANAGEMENT: ESSENTIAL STRATEGIES AND TOOLS 52
WORKFLOW AUTOMATION, DOCUMENT AUTOMATION, AND DUE DILIGENCE: LEGAL TECH SOLUTIONS 58
THE LEGAL TECH IMPLEMENTATION FRAMEWORK: KEY STEPS FOR SUCCESS 64
THE VALUE OF LEGAL TECH: MEASURING RETURN ON INVESTMENT (ROI) 69
DIY LEGAL TOOLS: FEATURES, BENEFITS, AND BEST USES 75
MASTERING DIY LEGAL TOOLS: E-SIGNING, DIGITAL SIGNATURES, AND DOCUMENT DRAFTING 82

ENHANCING LEGAL RESOURCE ACCESS: STRATEGIES AND BEST PRACTICES 87

LEGAL INFORMATION PORTALS: FEATURES, BENEFITS, AND USAGE TIPS 93

ONLINE DISPUTE RESOLUTION (ODR) UNCOVERED: BENEFITS AND KEY FEATURES 98

LEGAL CHATBOTS: FEATURES, BENEFITS, AND REAL-WORLD APPLICATIONS 104

LEGAL MARKETPLACES EXPLAINED: TYPES, BENEFITS, AND USES 109

DATA SCIENCE AND COMPUTATIONAL LAW: APPLICATIONS AND INNOVATIONS 114

ARTIFICIAL INTELLIGENCE (AI) IN LAW: KEY ASPECTS, APPLICATIONS, AND BENEFITS 119

ROBOT LAWYER, DIGITAL JUSTICE, AND VIRTUAL COURTS: UNDERSTANDING THE TECHNOLOGIES 124

VR AND AR IN LAW: TRANSFORMING LEGAL PRACTICE 129

BLOCKCHAIN AND SMART CONTRACTS PART 1: FUNDAMENTALS AND LEGAL APPLICATIONS 134

BLOCKCHAIN AND SMART CONTRACTS PART 2: ADVANCED APPLICATIONS IN LEGAL PRACTICE 140

KEY ETHICAL ISSUES IN LEGAL TECH AND ARTIFICIAL INTELLIGENCE (AI): AN IN-DEPTH LOOK 144

PROTECTING CLIENT INFORMATION: PRIVACY, CONFIDENTIALITY, AND CYBERSECURITY IN LAW 148

REAL-WORLD LEGAL CHALLENGES AND LESSONS LEARNED FROM: PRIVACY, CYBERSECURITY, AND UNAUTHORIZED PRACTICE 153

ADAPTING TO CHANGE: THE IMPACT OF TECHNOLOGY ON LEGAL CAREERS 157

UNDERSTANDING I-SHAPED, T-SHAPED, AND DELTA-SHAPED PROFESSIONALS 161

HOW TO DEVELOP A DIGITAL MINDSET FOR LEGAL SUCCESS 165

HOW TO TRANSFORM YOURSELF INTO A DIGITAL LEGAL PROFESSIONAL	170
USING DESIGN THINKING TO TRANSFORM YOUR LEGAL SERVICES	175
MASTERING LEGAL PROJECT MANAGEMENT (LPM): A COMPREHENSIVE GUIDE	180
UNDERSTANDING HOW LEGAL HACKATHONS ARE TRANSFORMING THE LEGAL INDUSTRY	185
LEGAL STARTUPS: SHAPING THE FUTURE OF THE LEGAL INDUSTRY	190
GENERATIVE AI (GAI) IN LAW: APPLICATIONS, BENEFITS, AND FUTURE TRENDS	195
HOW GENERATIVE AI IS REVOLUTIONIZING THE LEGAL LANDSCAPE	200
CONCLUSION	204
CHECK OUT OTHER BOOKS	205

INTRODUCTION

Welcome to the transformative world of legal technology and artificial intelligence. In an era where the legal landscape is being reshaped by rapid advancements, **"Mastering Legal Tech and AI"** is **your essential guide** to navigating and thriving in this new reality.

As we stand on the brink of a digital revolution, the legal profession is experiencing a seismic shift. The **tools, trends, and innovations** that once seemed futuristic are now indispensable in modern law practice and justice. From AI-driven legal research and predictive analytics to blockchain and smart contracts, the integration of technology is not just **enhancing efficiency**; it is fundamentally **altering the way legal services are delivered**.

This book is designed for lawyers, law students, and legal professionals who are eager to stay ahead of the curve. Whether you are a seasoned practitioner looking to incorporate the latest tech tools into your practice, a law student preparing for a tech-savvy legal career, or a professional aiming to understand the broader implications of these innovations, **this comprehensive guide offers valuable insights and practical advice**.

You will embark on a journey through the history and **evolution of legal tech**, exploring key milestones and groundbreaking technologies that have paved the way for today's advancements. We will delve into the diverse aspects of the legal tech landscape, from e-discovery and document automation to AI-driven legal analytics and online dispute resolution. Each chapter is crafted to provide a **deep understanding** of these tools and their **practical applications**, offering **strategies** to leverage them effectively in your practice.

But this book is more than just a technical manual. It is **a call to action** for the legal community to embrace change and innovation. As technology continues to evolve, so must our approach to law. The ability to adapt and integrate these tools will not only **enhance your efficiency and effectiveness** but also **open new avenues** for delivering justice and serving clients in ways previously unimaginable.

In the pages ahead, you will find **case studies, expert insights, and real-world applications** that illustrate the profound impact of legal tech and AI. We will also address the ethical considerations and challenges that come with these advancements, ensuring you are equipped to navigate the complexities of this digital transformation.

"Mastering Legal Tech and AI" is not just a book; it is **your roadmap to the future of law**. As you turn each page, we invite you to envision a legal practice that is smarter, more efficient, and more accessible. The future of law is here, and it is time to master it.

Join us on this exciting journey, and let's unlock the full potential of legal tech and AI together.

LEGAL TECH INTRODUCTION: WHY IT MATTERS AND HOW IT'S CHANGING LAW

Understanding Legal Tech

Legal Tech, short for "legal technology," refers to the use of technology and software to provide legal services and support the legal industry. This encompasses everything from tools that assist with legal research and document management to advanced solutions that utilize artificial intelligence (AI) and machine learning to automate legal tasks and improve efficiency. In this chapter, we will explore the basics of Legal Tech, its importance, and how it is transforming the legal landscape.

Simplifying Legal Tech

Imagine you have a stack of legal documents that need to be reviewed for relevant information. Traditionally, a lawyer or a team of paralegals would spend hours or even days going through these documents manually. With Legal Tech, sophisticated software can scan, categorize, and highlight important sections within minutes. This is just one example of how technology can streamline legal processes.

Legal Tech is not just about speed and efficiency; it also makes legal services more accessible. For instance, online platforms now allow individuals to create legal documents, such as wills or contracts, without the need for a lawyer. This democratizes access to legal services, making it easier and more affordable for everyone.

Key Components of Legal Tech

1. **Document Automation**: Tools that automatically generate legal documents based on templates and input data. For example, a small business owner can use document automation to create a legally binding contract by filling in a simple form online.

2. **Legal Research**: Advanced search tools that provide access to a vast database of legal precedents, statutes, and case law. A lawyer working on a complex case can quickly find relevant legal information using these tools, saving time and improving the quality of their work.

3. **Practice Management Software**: Systems that help law firms manage their day-to-day operations, including client management, billing, and scheduling. This type of software ensures that all aspects of a law firm's operations are running smoothly and efficiently.

4. **AI and Machine Learning**: Technologies that can analyze legal documents, predict case outcomes, and even assist in contract review by identifying potential risks and inconsistencies. For instance, an AI tool can review a non-disclosure agreement (NDA) and highlight any clauses that might be unfavorable to the signer.

5. **E-Discovery**: Software that assists in the identification, collection, and production of electronically stored information (ESI) for legal cases. This is crucial in litigation where relevant data may be scattered across multiple digital platforms.

6. **Online Dispute Resolution (ODR)**: Platforms that allow parties to resolve disputes through the internet, without needing to go to court. This can be particularly useful for small claims or disputes that are geographically spread out.

Why Legal Tech Matters

Legal Tech is revolutionizing the legal industry by making legal processes more efficient, reducing costs, and improving access to justice. Here are a few reasons why Legal Tech is becoming increasingly important:

1. **Cost Reduction**: Legal Tech helps law firms and legal departments cut costs by automating routine tasks and improving efficiency. This is especially important in an economic climate where clients are demanding more affordable legal services.

2. **Increased Efficiency**: Technology allows legal professionals to handle larger caseloads with greater accuracy and speed. For example, a lawyer using an AI-powered research tool can complete their research in a fraction of the time it would take using traditional methods.

3. **Accessibility**: By lowering the cost of legal services and providing online solutions, Legal Tech makes legal assistance available to a broader audience. This is particularly beneficial for individuals and small businesses who may not have the resources to hire traditional legal services.

4. **Innovation**: The rapid advancement of technology is driving innovation in the legal field. New tools and platforms are constantly being developed, offering legal professionals new ways to work and serve their clients.

Real-World Examples of Legal Tech in Action

Example 1: Document Automation

Scenario: Jane, a small business owner, needs to create a standard employment contract for her new employee.

Traditional Approach: Jane would need to hire a lawyer to draft the contract, which could be costly and time-consuming.

Legal Tech Solution: Using a document automation tool, Jane can generate a customized employment contract by filling out a simple online form. The tool ensures that the contract complies with current labor laws, and Jane can download and use the document immediately.

Example 2: AI-Powered Legal Research

Scenario: John, a lawyer, is preparing for a complex litigation case and needs to find relevant case law quickly.

Traditional Approach: John would spend hours manually searching through legal databases and books.

Legal Tech Solution: John uses an AI-powered legal research tool that scans thousands of legal documents and provides him with a list of relevant cases and statutes in minutes. This allows John to focus on developing his legal strategy rather than spending time on research.

Example 3: Online Dispute Resolution

Scenario: Sarah and Tom have a dispute over a business contract but live in different cities.

Traditional Approach: They would need to travel to court, which is expensive and time-consuming.

Legal Tech Solution: They use an online dispute resolution platform that allows them to resolve their conflict through video conferencing and digital document exchange. The platform provides a neutral mediator to help them reach an agreement, saving them time and money.

Conclusion

Legal Tech is transforming the legal industry by introducing tools and solutions that make legal services more efficient, accessible, and affordable. From document automation to AI-powered legal research, the possibilities are vast and continually expanding. As we continue to explore the world of Legal Tech, it is essential to stay informed about the latest trends and innovations that are shaping the future of law.

LEGAL TECH ADOPTION TODAY: TRENDS, INSIGHTS, AND FUTURE FORECASTS

The Current Landscape of Legal Tech

Legal Tech has rapidly evolved from a niche segment to a fundamental aspect of the legal industry. Today, law firms, legal departments, and even individual practitioners are increasingly turning to technology to improve efficiency, reduce costs, and enhance the quality of legal services. In this chapter, we will explore the current state of Legal Tech adoption, the emerging trends, and what the future holds for this dynamic field.

Why Understanding Legal Tech Adoption is Important

Understanding the trends in Legal Tech adoption is crucial for several reasons:

1. **Identifying High-Demand Technologies**: Knowing which technologies are currently in high demand helps legal professionals and businesses make informed decisions about which tools to invest in.
2. **Operational Insights**: By understanding where these technologies are being adopted, legal professionals can identify areas within their own practices that could benefit from tech integration.
3. **Career Development**: As Legal Tech continues to grow, new job roles and skill sets are emerging. Keeping up with these trends can help professionals stay competitive in the job market.
4. **Future-Proofing**: Anticipating future trends in Legal Tech allows legal professionals to prepare for upcoming changes and stay ahead of the curve.

Key Areas of Legal Tech Adoption

Legal Tech is now being utilized across various operational areas within the legal industry. Some of the most significant areas of adoption include:

1. **Legal Research and Case Management**: Advanced research tools and case management systems are helping legal professionals conduct thorough research more quickly and manage cases more efficiently. For example, AI-powered research tools like ROSS Intelligence can analyze large volumes of legal texts and provide relevant case law within seconds.
2. **Document Management and Automation**: Document automation tools, such as Contract Express, are transforming how legal documents are created

and managed. These tools enable law firms to generate complex legal documents quickly and accurately, reducing the time spent on manual drafting and review.

3. **E-Discovery**: E-discovery software, like Relativity, is becoming essential for handling large volumes of electronic data during litigation. These tools can sift through massive datasets to find relevant information, saving countless hours of manual document review.

4. **Billing and Financial Management**: Legal Tech solutions for billing and financial management, such as Clio, help law firms streamline their billing processes, manage client payments, and maintain financial records more effectively.

5. **Client Relationship Management (CRM)**: CRM tools designed for the legal industry, like Salesforce Legal, assist law firms in managing client interactions, tracking leads, and improving client service.

6. **Online Dispute Resolution (ODR)**: Platforms like Modria provide an alternative to traditional court proceedings by enabling parties to resolve disputes online. This can be particularly beneficial for small claims or disputes that are geographically spread out.

Current Trends in Legal Tech Adoption

Increased Use of AI and Machine Learning

Artificial intelligence and machine learning are at the forefront of Legal Tech innovation. These technologies are being used to automate routine tasks, such as document review and legal research, and to provide predictive analytics that can help legal professionals make better decisions.

Example: A law firm using AI to predict the outcome of litigation cases based on historical data, which allows them to advise clients more effectively and tailor their strategies accordingly.

Rise of Legal Tech Startups

The Legal Tech industry is witnessing a surge in the number of startups offering innovative solutions. These startups are often more agile than traditional law firms and can quickly bring new technologies to market.

Example: Companies like LegalZoom and Rocket Lawyer provide online legal services that are accessible and affordable, making it easier for individuals and small businesses to obtain legal help.

Growth of Cloud-Based Solutions

Cloud-based Legal Tech solutions are becoming increasingly popular due to their scalability, flexibility, and cost-effectiveness. These solutions enable legal professionals to access their tools and data from anywhere, facilitating remote work and collaboration.

Example: A law firm using a cloud-based case management system to allow lawyers to access case files and collaborate on documents from different locations.

Emphasis on Data Security and Privacy

With the increasing use of digital tools, data security and privacy have become major concerns in the legal industry. Legal Tech providers are investing heavily in security measures to protect sensitive information.

Example: Implementing robust encryption and secure access controls in a law firm's document management system to ensure client confidentiality.

Future Trends in Legal Tech

Expansion of AI Capabilities

As AI technology continues to advance, its applications in the legal industry are expected to expand. Future AI systems will likely be able to perform even more complex legal tasks, such as drafting legal arguments or providing real-time legal advice.

Example: A future AI tool that can analyze a case's legal merits and generate a draft of a legal brief, significantly reducing the time and effort required by human lawyers.

Integration of Blockchain Technology

Blockchain technology is poised to revolutionize the legal industry by providing secure, transparent, and tamper-proof records of transactions and legal documents. This could be particularly useful for areas such as contract management and intellectual property rights.

Example: Using blockchain to create a smart contract that automatically executes the terms of an agreement when certain conditions are met, without the need for manual intervention.

Development of Legal Tech Ecosystems

The future of Legal Tech will likely see the development of integrated ecosystems that combine various technologies to provide comprehensive solutions for legal professionals. These ecosystems will offer end-to-end services that cover all aspects of legal practice, from client intake to case resolution.

Example: An integrated Legal Tech platform that combines case management, document automation, and AI-powered legal research, providing a one-stop solution for law firms.

Emergence of New Job Roles

As Legal Tech continues to evolve, new job roles will emerge that require a combination of legal knowledge and technological expertise. These roles will be crucial for bridging the gap between traditional legal practice and modern technology.

Example: A legal data scientist who specializes in analyzing large datasets to uncover trends and insights that can inform legal strategies.

Conclusion

The adoption of Legal Tech is transforming the legal industry, making it more efficient, accessible, and future-ready. By staying informed about current trends and anticipating future developments, legal professionals can position themselves to take advantage of the opportunities that Legal Tech offers. In the next chapter, we will explore the historical development of Legal Tech and how it has evolved to its current state.

EXPLORE THE HISTORY OF LEGAL TECH: KEY MILESTONES AND TECHNOLOGIES THAT HAVE DEFINED ITS DEVELOPMENT

The Beginnings of Legal Tech

The journey of Legal Tech is a fascinating tale of innovation and gradual transformation. From the early dreams of automation to the sophisticated AI-driven tools of today, the evolution of Legal Tech has reshaped the legal landscape, making legal services more efficient and accessible. In this chapter, we will explore the history of Legal Tech, highlighting key milestones and technologies that have defined its development.

The Early Visionaries

The concept of Legal Tech can be traced back to the 17th century when the German philosopher and mathematician, Gottfried Wilhelm Leibniz, envisioned a system where legal judgments could be derived from a logical calculation, much like solving a mathematical problem. This idea, known as the "Leibniz Dream," aimed to make law as precise as mathematics by using logic and computation(1111).

Although Leibniz's vision was far ahead of its time, it laid the groundwork for the idea that legal processes could be streamlined and improved through automation.

The Advent of Digital Legal Research

The first significant step towards realizing the Leibniz Dream came in the 1970s with the development of online legal research tools. In Canada, Quicklaw was established as the first online legal research project by Professor Hugh Lawford at Queen's University. Around the same time in the United States, LexisNexis introduced a mainframe computer system, Ubik, which allowed lawyers to search for case law electronically(1111).

Example: Imagine being a lawyer in the 1970s, needing to spend countless hours in a law library, manually searching through volumes of case law. With Quicklaw and LexisNexis, you could now access the same information in a fraction of the time, directly from your office.

The Rise of Personal Computers and Word Processing

The 1980s marked a significant turning point with the introduction of personal computers and word processing software in law firms. This technology revolutionized the way legal documents were created and managed. Lawyers could now draft, edit, and store documents electronically, which greatly improved productivity.

Example: Before word processors, drafting a legal document required typing it out manually or dictating it to a secretary. Corrections and revisions were cumbersome. With word processors, changes could be made quickly and easily, allowing for faster turnaround times.

Legal Tech in the 1990s: Connectivity and Communication

The 1990s saw the widespread adoption of personal computers and the rise of networked environments in law firms. This period also witnessed the advent of email and other electronic communication tools, which facilitated faster and more efficient communication between lawyers and clients.

Example: A lawyer could now send an email with an attached legal document to a client for review, rather than relying on traditional mail services, significantly speeding up the exchange of information.

The Emergence of DIY Legal Services

The early 2000s brought about a new wave of innovation with the launch of online DIY legal services. LegalZoom, founded in 2001, was a pioneer in this field, offering a platform where users could create legal documents such as wills and contracts without needing to hire a lawyer(1111).

Example: A small business owner needing to draft a partnership agreement could use LegalZoom to generate a legally binding document by simply providing the necessary details online, saving time and legal fees.

The Virtual Law Firm and E-Discovery

In 2002, FisherBroyles became the first virtual law firm, operating without a traditional brick-and-mortar office. This innovative model reduced overhead costs and provided more flexible working conditions for lawyers(1111).

The mid-2000s also saw the rise of e-discovery, a process that involves collecting and analyzing electronic data for legal cases. Tools like Relativity became essential for handling large volumes of digital information, making the discovery process more efficient.

Example: During a litigation case, a lawyer could use e-discovery software to search through thousands of emails and documents to find relevant evidence, a task that would be nearly impossible to accomplish manually.

The Impact of Mobile Technology and Cloud Computing

The late 2000s witnessed the explosion of mobile technology and the rise of cloud computing. Lawyers could now access case files, legal research, and other resources from their smartphones and tablets, enabling them to work from virtually anywhere.

Example: A lawyer traveling for a court appearance could review case notes and legal research on their tablet during the flight, ensuring they were well-prepared upon arrival.

Cloud computing also revolutionized how legal services were delivered. Software-as-a-service (SaaS) models allowed law firms to access powerful legal tools without needing to invest in expensive hardware and software.

The Evolution of Legal Marketplaces

Platforms like Avvo, launched in 2007, and Rocket Lawyer, founded in 2008, transformed how people accessed legal services. These platforms provided marketplaces where individuals could find and hire lawyers, read reviews, and even access basic legal services online(1111).

Example: Someone needing legal advice could use Avvo to search for a lawyer in their area, read client reviews, and even ask legal questions online, making it easier to find reliable legal help.

The Present and Future of Legal Tech

Today, Legal Tech is an integral part of the legal industry. From AI-powered research tools to blockchain-based smart contracts, the technologies available are more advanced and accessible than ever before. Legal professionals are using these tools to streamline workflows, reduce costs, and improve service delivery.

The Role of AI and Machine Learning

Artificial intelligence and machine learning are playing a significant role in the current landscape of Legal Tech. These technologies are being used to automate document review, predict case outcomes, and even draft legal documents.

Example: A law firm could use an AI tool to review thousands of contracts, identify common clauses, and highlight any potential risks, significantly reducing the time and effort required by human lawyers.

The Rise of Legal Chatbots

Legal chatbots are becoming increasingly popular for providing basic legal advice and information. These tools use AI to understand and respond to legal queries, making legal advice more accessible to the general public.

Example: A chatbot on a law firm's website could answer common legal questions, such as how to file for divorce or what steps to take when starting a business, providing valuable information without the need for a lawyer's direct involvement.

Conclusion

The history of Legal Tech is a story of continuous innovation and progress. From the early dreams of automating legal processes to the sophisticated technologies of today, Legal Tech has transformed the legal industry, making it more efficient, accessible, and forward-thinking. As we move into the future, the role of technology in law will only continue to grow, bringing new opportunities and challenges for legal professionals.

UNDERSTANDING THE VARIOUS ASPECTS OF THE LEGAL TECH LANDSCAPE

Introduction

Welcome to the ever-evolving landscape of Legal Tech! Legal Tech encompasses a broad spectrum of technologies designed to support and enhance the delivery of legal services. Understanding this landscape is crucial for anyone in the legal field, from beginners to seasoned professionals, as it provides a comprehensive view of the tools and technologies transforming legal practice. In this chapter, we will explore the various aspects of the Legal Tech landscape, including its key components, the technologies driving change, and practical examples of how these tools are used in real-world scenarios.

Understanding the Legal Tech Landscape

The Legal Tech landscape can be viewed from multiple perspectives, each offering a unique insight into the technologies and solutions available:

1. **Operations Perspective**: This viewpoint focuses on the technologies that streamline and automate various legal tasks and processes.
2. **Technology Type**: Examines the types of technologies, such as artificial intelligence (AI) and blockchain, that are used in legal service delivery.
3. **Product Viewpoint**: Looks at the specific Legal Tech products available in the market.
4. **Market Perspective**: Considers the companies and organizations developing these technologies.
5. **Customer Perspective**: Focuses on the users of these technologies, including lawyers, individuals, businesses, and the judiciary(1111).

Key Components of the Legal Tech Landscape

The Legal Tech landscape is diverse and includes several key components, each addressing different aspects of legal practice:

1. **Document Automation**: Tools that help automate the creation, management, and storage of legal documents.
2. **E-Discovery**: Software that assists in the identification, collection, and production of electronically stored information (ESI) for legal cases.

3. **Legal Research**: Advanced tools that provide access to legal precedents, statutes, and case law.
4. **Practice Management**: Systems that help law firms manage their day-to-day operations.
5. **Client Relationship Management (CRM)**: Tools that assist in managing client interactions and tracking leads.
6. **Online Dispute Resolution (ODR)**: Platforms that allow parties to resolve disputes through the internet.

Exploring the Technologies

Artificial Intelligence and Machine Learning

AI and machine learning are revolutionizing legal services by automating routine tasks, improving efficiency, and providing predictive analytics.

Example: A law firm uses AI to review large volumes of contracts, identifying potential risks and inconsistencies that might otherwise be missed during manual review.

Blockchain Technology

Blockchain offers secure, transparent, and tamper-proof records of transactions and legal documents, which can be particularly useful for contract management and intellectual property.

Example: Using blockchain to create smart contracts that automatically execute when conditions are met, eliminating the need for intermediaries.

Cloud Computing

Cloud computing allows legal professionals to access data and applications from anywhere, facilitating remote work and collaboration.

Example: A law firm uses a cloud-based case management system to enable lawyers to access case files and collaborate on documents from different locations.

E-Discovery Tools

E-discovery tools are essential for managing the large volumes of electronic data that are increasingly part of legal cases.

Example: An attorney uses e-discovery software to quickly search through thousands of emails and documents to find relevant evidence for a case.

Online Dispute Resolution (ODR)

ODR platforms enable parties to resolve disputes online, providing a more accessible and cost-effective alternative to traditional court proceedings.

Example: Two businesses in different countries use an ODR platform to resolve a contract dispute without the need for expensive international litigation.

Practical Examples of Legal Tech

Document Automation in Practice

Scenario: A startup needs to draft a series of employment contracts quickly as it scales up its operations.

Traditional Approach: The startup would need to hire a lawyer to draft each contract, a time-consuming and costly process.

Legal Tech Solution: Using a document automation tool like Contract Express, the startup can generate customized employment contracts by filling out a simple online form, saving time and reducing legal fees.

AI-Powered Legal Research

Scenario: A law firm is preparing for a complex litigation case and needs to conduct extensive legal research.

Traditional Approach: Researchers would manually sift through volumes of case law and legal texts, a process that could take weeks.

Legal Tech Solution: Using an AI-powered research tool like ROSS Intelligence, the firm can quickly analyze a vast database of legal documents and find relevant case law in a matter of minutes.

Online Dispute Resolution in Action

Scenario: Two individuals have a dispute over a contract and are looking for a quick resolution without going to court.

Traditional Approach: They would need to hire lawyers and possibly go through a lengthy court process.

Legal Tech Solution: They use an ODR platform like Modria to resolve their dispute online, which is faster, cheaper, and less stressful than traditional litigation.

The Future of Legal Tech

The Legal Tech landscape is continually evolving, with new technologies and innovations emerging regularly. The future of Legal Tech promises further integration of AI, greater adoption of blockchain for secure transactions, and increased reliance on cloud computing for remote legal services.

Anticipated Trends

- **Expansion of AI Capabilities**: AI will continue to advance, offering more sophisticated tools for tasks like legal drafting and predictive analytics.
- **Growth of Blockchain Applications**: Blockchain technology will become more prevalent, particularly in areas like smart contracts and secure document storage.
- **Increased Use of Cloud-Based Solutions**: More law firms and legal departments will adopt cloud-based systems for their flexibility and scalability.

Conclusion

Understanding the Legal Tech landscape is essential for anyone involved in the legal profession. By exploring the key components, technologies, and practical applications of Legal Tech, you can gain a comprehensive view of how technology is transforming the legal industry and preparing for future developments. In the next chapter, we will delve into specific Legal Tech tools and how they can be integrated into legal practice to enhance efficiency and service delivery.

LEGAL SERVICE DELIVERY: EXPLORE DIVERSE APPROACHES AND BENEFITS

Introduction to Legal Service Delivery

Legal service delivery is the process through which legal services are provided to clients. It encompasses a wide range of activities, from in-person consultations and court appearances to online legal marketplaces and automated systems. The goal of effective legal service delivery is to provide clients with convenient, efficient, and cost-effective access to legal services while maintaining high ethical and professional standards. In this chapter, we will explore the various methods of delivering legal services, the technologies that are transforming this process, and practical examples of how these innovations are being applied in the real world.

Methods of Legal Service Delivery

In-Person Delivery

In-person delivery of legal services involves direct interaction between clients and legal professionals. This traditional method includes consultations, court appearances, and face-to-face meetings.

Example: A lawyer meets with a client in their office to discuss the details of a legal case, providing personalized advice and representation in court.

Online Delivery

Online delivery of legal services uses digital platforms to offer legal advice and assistance. This method can range from virtual consultations to automated legal document creation.

Example: An individual uses an online platform like LegalZoom to create a legally binding will by following a guided process and filling out necessary information online.

Hybrid Delivery

Hybrid delivery combines in-person and online methods, offering a flexible approach to legal service delivery that can be tailored to the needs of the client.

Example: A client consults with a lawyer via video conference for initial advice and then meets in person for more detailed discussions and document signing.

Key Elements of Legal Service Delivery

Legal service delivery involves several key elements, each contributing to the overall efficiency and effectiveness of the service provided.

Practice Management

Practice management involves the consolidation of administrative tasks into a single dashboard using case management solutions. This helps legal professionals streamline both their legal and operational processes.

Example: A law firm uses practice management software like Clio to manage client information, schedule appointments, and track billable hours in one integrated system.

Research and Analytics

Research and analytics tools analyze archives of case decisions and legal documents to produce useful insights for legal professionals. This helps in preparation, arguments, and predictions about case outcomes.

Example: A lawyer uses a legal research tool like LexisNexis to find relevant case law and statutes that support their client's case.

Case Management

Case management enables legal professionals to monitor all their engagements on a unified platform. This includes client onboarding, case preparation, real-time tracking of updates, and periodic client communications.

Example: A lawyer uses case management software to track the progress of multiple cases, ensuring that deadlines are met and clients are kept informed about their case status.

Evidence Management

Evidence management involves gathering, analyzing, and preserving vital evidence for legal cases. This is crucial for both law enforcement agencies and corporate investigations.

Example: An e-discovery tool is used to sift through thousands of emails and documents to find relevant evidence for a corporate litigation case.

Court Management

Court management aims to enhance the efficiency and effectiveness of court administration by promoting an interconnected judiciary and enabling automation of court processes.

Example: An online court management system allows lawyers to file documents electronically and track the status of court cases in real-time.

The Role of Technology in Legal Service Delivery

Technology plays a pivotal role in modernizing and improving the delivery of legal services. Here are some key technologies that are shaping the legal landscape:

Document Automation

Document automation tools streamline the creation and management of legal documents, reducing the time and effort required to draft and review paperwork.

Example: A lawyer uses document automation software to generate a series of standardized contracts for a client, ensuring consistency and accuracy across all documents.

Artificial Intelligence (AI)

AI is used to automate routine tasks, such as legal research and document review, and to provide predictive analytics that help legal professionals make informed decisions.

Example: An AI tool reviews a set of legal documents for a due diligence process, identifying any clauses that might pose a risk to the client.

Online Dispute Resolution (ODR)

ODR platforms allow parties to resolve disputes through the internet, providing a convenient and cost-effective alternative to traditional court proceedings.

Example: Two businesses use an ODR platform to settle a contractual dispute without the need for costly litigation.

Cloud Computing

Cloud computing enables legal professionals to access their tools and data from anywhere, facilitating remote work and collaboration.

Example: A law firm uses a cloud-based case management system to allow lawyers to work on cases from different locations and devices.

Blockchain Technology

Blockchain provides secure, transparent, and tamper-proof records of transactions and legal documents, which is particularly useful for contract management and intellectual property.

Example: A blockchain-based smart contract automatically executes the terms of an agreement once certain conditions are met, without the need for manual intervention.

Client Relationship Management (CRM)

CRM tools help law firms manage client interactions, track leads, and improve client service.

Example: A law firm uses a CRM system to keep track of client communications and follow up on potential leads, improving client retention and satisfaction.

Practical Examples of Legal Service Delivery Innovations

Example 1: Virtual Law Firms

Scenario: A law firm operates without a traditional office, offering services entirely online.

Traditional Approach: Clients would need to visit a physical office for consultations and document signing.

Legal Tech Solution: The virtual law firm uses video conferencing, electronic document signing, and cloud-based case management to provide a full range of legal services remotely, reducing overhead costs and providing greater flexibility for both clients and lawyers.

Example 2: Automated Legal Document Creation

Scenario: An entrepreneur needs to create a series of contracts for their new business quickly.

Traditional Approach: The entrepreneur would hire a lawyer to draft each contract individually, which could be time-consuming and expensive.

Legal Tech Solution: Using a document automation tool, the entrepreneur can generate customized contracts by filling out a simple online form, saving time and reducing legal fees.

Example 3: Online Legal Marketplaces

Scenario: An individual needs legal advice but does not have a regular lawyer.

Traditional Approach: The individual would need to find and hire a lawyer through traditional means, such as referrals or advertisements.

Legal Tech Solution: The individual uses an online legal marketplace like Avvo to search for lawyers, read reviews, and even get answers to basic legal questions, making it easier to find and hire legal help.

Conclusion

The landscape of legal service delivery is undergoing significant changes, driven by advancements in technology. By understanding the various methods and technologies involved in legal service delivery, legal professionals can improve their efficiency, reduce costs, and provide better service to their clients. In the next chapter, we will delve into specific legal technologies and tools that are transforming the legal industry and explore how they can be integrated into legal practice to enhance service delivery and client satisfaction.

PRACTICAL APPLICATIONS OF LEGAL TECH: HOW TECHNOLOGY IS SHAPING LEGAL PRACTICE

Introduction to Legal Tech in Use

Welcome to the practical world of Legal Tech! This chapter focuses on how various technologies are being utilized in real-world legal settings to enhance the efficiency, effectiveness, and accessibility of legal services. We will explore specific examples of Legal Tech in action across different areas of law, providing a comprehensive overview of the tools and technologies that are transforming the legal profession. This guide is designed to be easy to understand, even for beginners, and aims to equip you with the knowledge to navigate the modern legal landscape effectively.

Key Areas of Legal Tech Application

Legal Tech is being applied across a wide range of areas within the legal profession. Here, we will explore some of the key areas where Legal Tech is making a significant impact:

1. Document Automation

Document automation tools are revolutionizing the way legal documents are created, managed, and stored. These tools help reduce the time and effort required to draft legal documents, ensuring consistency and accuracy.

Example: A law firm uses document automation software to generate a series of standard contracts for a new client. By inputting specific client details into a template, the software automatically produces customized contracts, saving hours of manual drafting.

Illustration:

- **Tool**: HotDocs
- **Usage**: A lawyer inputs client-specific data into a form, and HotDocs generates a legally compliant contract, reducing the time spent on document preparation from hours to minutes.

2. E-Discovery

E-discovery tools assist in the identification, collection, and production of electronically stored information (ESI) for legal cases. These tools are crucial for managing large volumes of digital data during litigation.

Example: During a complex litigation case, a legal team uses an e-discovery tool to sift through thousands of emails and documents to find relevant evidence. This significantly reduces the time required for manual document review and ensures that no critical information is overlooked.

Illustration:

- **Tool**: Relativity
- **Usage**: The tool helps a legal team filter through a massive dataset to identify emails and documents that are relevant to the case, expediting the discovery process and improving accuracy.

3. Legal Research and Analytics

Advanced legal research tools provide access to vast databases of legal texts, case law, and statutes, allowing legal professionals to conduct thorough research more efficiently.

Example: A lawyer preparing for a trial uses an AI-powered legal research tool to find relevant case law and legal precedents. This tool helps identify key legal arguments and case outcomes, providing a strategic advantage.

Illustration:

- **Tool**: LexisNexis
- **Usage**: A lawyer uses LexisNexis to search for and retrieve relevant legal precedents, statutes, and case summaries, ensuring they have the necessary legal foundation for their case.

4. Practice Management

Practice management software helps law firms streamline their operations by managing client information, scheduling appointments, tracking billable hours, and storing legal documents.

Example: A law firm uses practice management software to coordinate tasks, manage client communications, and ensure that all cases are progressing smoothly. This tool helps the firm operate more efficiently and improve client service.

Illustration:

- **Tool**: Clio

- **Usage**: The firm uses Clio to manage client details, schedule meetings, and track billable hours, integrating all aspects of case management into a single platform.

5. Online Dispute Resolution (ODR)

ODR platforms enable parties to resolve disputes online, providing a more accessible and cost-effective alternative to traditional court proceedings.

Example: Two businesses in different countries use an ODR platform to resolve a contractual dispute. This allows them to settle their differences without the need for expensive and time-consuming litigation.

Illustration:

- **Tool**: Modria
- **Usage**: The businesses use Modria to negotiate and resolve their dispute online, avoiding the costs and delays associated with traditional legal processes.

Detailed Examples of Legal Tech Tools in Use

Example 1: LegalZoom for Document Automation

Scenario: A small business owner needs to create an employment contract for a new hire quickly and cost-effectively.

Traditional Approach: The business owner would typically need to hire a lawyer to draft the contract, which could be both expensive and time-consuming.

Legal Tech Solution: The owner uses LegalZoom to create a customized employment contract by following a step-by-step online process. The platform provides a template that the owner can modify to fit their specific needs.

Outcome: The owner obtains a legally binding contract in a matter of minutes, saving both time and legal fees.

Example 2: Relativity for E-Discovery

Scenario: A law firm is handling a large-scale litigation case that involves reviewing thousands of electronic documents to find relevant evidence.

Traditional Approach: The firm would have to manually review each document, a process that could take weeks or even months.

Legal Tech Solution: The firm uses Relativity to automate the e-discovery process. The tool scans and categorizes the documents, highlighting those that are relevant to the case.

Outcome: The firm completes the document review process in a fraction of the time, ensuring that no critical evidence is missed and that the case is prepared more efficiently.

Example 3: LexisNexis for Legal Research

Scenario: A lawyer needs to prepare a legal brief and requires comprehensive research on relevant case law and statutes.

Traditional Approach: The lawyer would spend hours or days manually searching through legal databases and books.

Legal Tech Solution: The lawyer uses LexisNexis to quickly search for and retrieve relevant legal texts, case law, and statutes, all from a single platform.

Outcome: The lawyer completes their research in a much shorter time, allowing them to focus more on building a strong legal argument.

Example 4: Clio for Practice Management

Scenario: A law firm is struggling to manage its workload and client communications efficiently.

Traditional Approach: The firm would rely on multiple, disconnected systems to manage client information, schedule appointments, and track billable hours.

Legal Tech Solution: The firm adopts Clio, an integrated practice management software that consolidates all these tasks into a single platform.

Outcome: The firm operates more smoothly, with improved client communication and more accurate tracking of billable hours, leading to better overall efficiency and client satisfaction.

Example 5: Modria for Online Dispute Resolution

Scenario: Two companies are involved in a dispute over a contract and want to resolve the issue without going to court.

Traditional Approach: The companies would hire lawyers and potentially go through a lengthy court process.

Legal Tech Solution: They use Modria, an ODR platform, to negotiate and resolve their dispute online.

Outcome: The dispute is resolved more quickly and at a lower cost than traditional litigation, and both parties are able to move forward without the stress of a prolonged legal battle.

Benefits of Legal Tech in Practice

Efficiency

Legal Tech tools significantly reduce the time required to complete legal tasks, from document preparation to case management, allowing legal professionals to focus more on their clients and less on administrative work.

Cost Savings

By automating routine tasks and streamlining workflows, Legal Tech helps reduce operational costs, making legal services more affordable and accessible to a broader range of clients.

Accessibility

Online platforms and cloud-based solutions make legal services accessible to people who might not have the means or opportunity to visit a law office in person.

Accuracy and Compliance

Automated tools ensure that legal documents are prepared accurately and in compliance with relevant laws and regulations, reducing the risk of errors and legal issues.

Conclusion

Legal Tech is playing an increasingly important role in the delivery of legal services, offering tools and technologies that enhance efficiency, reduce costs, and improve access to legal assistance. By understanding how these tools are used in practice, legal professionals can leverage them to provide better service to their clients and stay competitive in a rapidly changing legal landscape. In the next chapter, we will explore the ethical and practical considerations of implementing Legal Tech in legal practice.

E-DISCOVERY ESSENTIALS: KEY COMPONENTS AND PRACTICAL INSIGHTS

Introduction to e-Discovery

Welcome to the fascinating world of e-Discovery! As a critical component of modern legal practice, e-Discovery involves the process of identifying, collecting, and analyzing electronically stored information (ESI) for use as evidence in legal cases. Understanding e-Discovery is essential for legal professionals, as it enables them to manage large volumes of digital data efficiently and effectively. In this chapter, we will explore the fundamentals of e-Discovery, its key components, and practical examples of how it is used in real-world scenarios. Our goal is to make this topic accessible to beginners while providing a detailed, professional overview.

What is e-Discovery?

e-Discovery, short for electronic discovery, refers to the process of locating, securing, and examining electronic data that may be relevant to a legal case. This data can include emails, documents, databases, audio and video files, social media posts, and more. The primary objective of e-Discovery is to gather this information in a way that is legally admissible and useful for litigation or investigation.

Difference Between e-Discovery and Computer Forensics

While e-Discovery focuses on gathering active data and metadata from electronic sources, computer forensics delves deeper into hidden folders and unallocated disk spaces to uncover details of specific events or incidents. e-Discovery is concerned with data that is readily accessible and available, whereas computer forensics aims to uncover hidden or deleted data.

Example: In a corporate fraud case, e-Discovery might involve collecting emails and financial records to establish a timeline of events, while computer forensics would be used to recover deleted files that might reveal tampering with financial statements.

Key Components of e-Discovery

Active Data and Metadata

Active data includes the actual contents of electronic files, such as text in a document or the body of an email. Metadata, on the other hand, is descriptive information embedded within an electronic file, such as the author, creation date, and file history.

Example: An email's active data would be the message text and attachments, while metadata would include the sender's and recipient's email addresses, the date and time the email was sent, and the email's path through servers.

Electronically Stored Information (ESI)

ESI encompasses any data created, stored, or transmitted in digital form, including emails, documents, databases, audio and video files, and social media posts. ESI is stored on various devices, such as computers, servers, smartphones, and cloud storage services.

Example: A company might have ESI on its servers that include email correspondence, business documents, and customer databases, all of which could be relevant in a legal case.

The e-Discovery Process

e-Discovery involves several stages, often described by the Electronic Discovery Reference Model (EDRM). These stages include:

1. Information Governance

This stage involves understanding an organization's data footprint and creating a plan to control it. Effective information governance helps ensure that relevant data is available for e-Discovery when needed.

Example: A company implements a data retention policy to ensure that important emails and documents are preserved and easily accessible for potential legal matters.

2. Identification

In this stage, potential sources of relevant information are identified. This includes determining which devices, databases, and communication platforms may contain data pertinent to the case.

Example: During an investigation, a legal team identifies that relevant information is stored on the company's email server and cloud storage system.

3. Preservation

This involves ensuring that the identified data is preserved in its original form to prevent alteration or deletion. Legal holds are often placed on data to maintain its integrity.

Example: A court issues a legal hold on a company's email server, requiring the company to preserve all emails related to a pending lawsuit.

4. Collection

Data is forensically collected from various sources to ensure that it can be used as evidence. This step involves extracting data in a way that maintains its authenticity and chain of custody.

Example: A forensic team collects data from a company's email server, including messages, attachments, and metadata, for use in a legal case.

5. Processing

The collected data is processed to reduce its volume and isolate relevant information. This often involves filtering out duplicate files and irrelevant data.

Example: A legal team uses e-Discovery software to process thousands of emails, removing duplicates and identifying messages relevant to the case.

6. Review

In this stage, the processed data is reviewed to identify relevant documents and information. Legal professionals assess the data for relevance, privilege, and confidentiality.

Example: Lawyers review the collected emails to determine which ones contain information pertinent to the case and which are protected by attorney-client privilege.

7. Analysis

Data is analyzed to uncover patterns, relationships, and key facts that can support the case. This may involve examining communication threads, document versions, and other contextual information.

Example: Analysts examine email threads to identify key conversations and timeline events that are critical to the case.

8. Production

Relevant data is produced in a format suitable for use in litigation, such as PDFs or TIFF files. This step involves preparing data for presentation in court or for sharing with other parties.

Example: The legal team produces a set of emails and documents in PDF format to be submitted as evidence in court.

9. Presentation

The final stage involves presenting the digital evidence in court or other legal settings. This may include creating exhibits, reports, and other visual aids to support the case.

Example: During a trial, lawyers present key emails and documents to the court, using digital exhibits to illustrate their arguments.

Practical Examples of e-Discovery in Action

Example 1: Corporate Fraud Investigation

Scenario: A company suspects that an employee has been embezzling funds and needs to gather evidence for a legal case.

Traditional Approach: The company would manually search through financial records and emails, a time-consuming and potentially incomplete process.

e-Discovery Solution: The company uses e-Discovery software to collect and analyze emails, financial documents, and transaction records. The software identifies suspicious activity, such as unauthorized transfers and email communications discussing the scheme.

Outcome: The company quickly gathers comprehensive evidence to support its case against the employee, leading to a successful prosecution.

Example 2: Intellectual Property Dispute

Scenario: Two companies are involved in a dispute over patent infringement and need to review large volumes of technical documents and communications.

Traditional Approach: Both parties would manually review documents and emails to find relevant information, a labor-intensive process.

e-Discovery Solution: e-Discovery tools are used to collect and review emails, technical documents, and design files. The software helps identify key documents and communications that demonstrate patent infringement.

Outcome: The companies are able to efficiently review large volumes of data, identify critical evidence, and resolve the dispute through negotiation or litigation.

Example 3: Employment Litigation

Scenario: An employee files a lawsuit against their employer, claiming wrongful termination based on discriminatory practices.

Traditional Approach: The employer would need to manually gather and review personnel files, emails, and other documents to build their defense.

e-Discovery Solution: The employer uses e-Discovery software to collect and analyze emails, performance reviews, and HR records. The software helps identify documents and communications relevant to the employee's claims.

Outcome: The employer efficiently gathers and reviews evidence to support their defense, leading to a more informed legal strategy.

Benefits of e-Discovery

Efficiency

e-Discovery tools significantly reduce the time required to collect, process, and review large volumes of electronic data, allowing legal professionals to focus on case strategy rather than data management.

Cost Savings

By automating the e-Discovery process, legal teams can reduce the costs associated with manual data collection and review, making litigation more affordable.

Accuracy and Compliance

e-Discovery ensures that relevant data is collected and preserved in a legally compliant manner, reducing the risk of missing critical evidence or facing sanctions for spoliation.

Enhanced Data Analysis

e-Discovery tools provide advanced analytics capabilities, enabling legal professionals to uncover patterns and insights that may be crucial to their case.

Choosing the Right e-Discovery Tools

When selecting e-Discovery tools, consider the following factors:

Ease of Use

Choose software that is intuitive and user-friendly, allowing legal teams to quickly get up to speed and use the tools effectively.

Integration

Look for tools that integrate well with other technologies, such as case management systems and legal databases, to ensure a seamless workflow.

Flexibility

Select tools that offer flexible deployment options, such as cloud-based or on-premises solutions, to meet the specific needs of your organization.

Support

Ensure that the vendor provides responsive support and training to help you maximize the effectiveness of the e-Discovery tools.

Conclusion

e-Discovery is a vital part of modern legal practice, enabling legal professionals to efficiently manage the growing volumes of digital data involved in litigation and investigations. By understanding the key components and processes of e-Discovery, and by using the right tools, legal teams can enhance their ability to gather and present evidence, ultimately improving their chances of success in legal matters. In the next chapter, we will explore the role of legal research and analytics in modern legal practice.

LEGAL RESEARCH AND ANALYTICS: ESSENTIAL TOOLS AND TECHNIQUES

Introduction to Legal Research and Analytics

Legal research and analytics are fundamental components of modern legal practice. These skills enable legal professionals to collect, analyze, and interpret relevant information, supporting effective legal arguments and decision-making. With the advent of digital tools and vast online databases, legal research has undergone a significant transformation, requiring professionals to be adept at using these resources. Legal analytics, meanwhile, leverages data and statistical analysis to uncover patterns and provide insights, helping legal practitioners make informed decisions, anticipate outcomes, and identify potential risks.

In this chapter, we will explore the essentials of legal research and analytics, the tools and technologies that support these activities, and practical examples of how they are used in real-world scenarios. Our goal is to make this topic accessible and understandable for beginners, while providing a comprehensive and professional overview.

The Evolution of Legal Research and Analytics

Traditional Legal Research

Traditionally, legal research involved manually searching through physical law libraries, case law books, statutes, and legal journals. This process was time-consuming and required significant effort to locate relevant information.

Example: A lawyer preparing for a case would spend hours in a law library, searching through books and journals to find precedents and legal statutes that supported their argument.

Modern Legal Research

Today, digital tools and online databases have revolutionized legal research. These resources provide quick and easy access to vast amounts of legal information, allowing legal professionals to conduct research more efficiently and effectively.

Example: Using an online legal research platform like Westlaw, a lawyer can quickly search for relevant case law, statutes, and legal articles, saving time and ensuring comprehensive research.

The Rise of Legal Analytics

Legal analytics involves the use of data and statistical analysis to identify trends, patterns, and insights within legal data. This approach enables legal professionals to make data-driven decisions and anticipate legal outcomes.

Example: A legal team uses analytics to analyze past case outcomes and identify factors that influence the likelihood of success in similar cases, helping them develop more effective legal strategies.

Key Tools for Legal Research and Analytics

Online Legal Research Platforms

Online legal research platforms provide access to a comprehensive database of legal texts, case law, and statutes. These platforms often include advanced search functionalities and tools for organizing and analyzing information.

Example: LexisNexis is a popular legal research platform that offers extensive legal databases, search tools, and analytics features, enabling users to quickly find and analyze legal information.

Legal Analytics Software

Legal analytics software uses data analysis techniques to provide insights into legal data. These tools can analyze large datasets, identify trends, and generate reports that support legal decision-making.

Example: Lex Machina is a legal analytics tool that analyzes litigation data to provide insights into case outcomes, helping lawyers assess the strengths and weaknesses of their cases.

Techniques in Legal Research and Analytics

Information Extraction

Information extraction involves identifying relevant data points within a larger body of text or data. This technique helps legal professionals quickly locate and analyze important information.

Example: A lawyer uses a text-mining tool to extract key terms and phrases from a large collection of legal documents, identifying the most relevant information for their case.

Data Visualization

Data visualization represents complex data in a more accessible and digestible format, such as graphs, charts, or heatmaps. This helps legal professionals identify trends, patterns, or anomalies that may not be apparent from text-based analysis.

Example: A legal analyst uses data visualization to create a graph that shows trends in case outcomes over time, making it easier to identify significant patterns.

Anomaly Detection

Anomaly detection identifies irregularities or unusual patterns within data that may indicate issues such as fraud or non-compliance. This technique is particularly useful for identifying and mitigating risks.

Example: A law firm uses anomaly detection algorithms to analyze financial transactions and identify unusual patterns that could indicate fraudulent activity.

Practical Applications of Legal Research and Analytics

Case Law Research

Scenario: A lawyer is preparing for a trial and needs to find relevant case law to support their arguments.

Traditional Approach: The lawyer would manually search through law books and legal journals, a process that could take days or weeks.

Modern Approach: Using an online legal research platform like Westlaw, the lawyer can quickly search for relevant case law, review summaries, and download full-text documents, significantly reducing research time.

Outcome: The lawyer is able to conduct thorough research in a fraction of the time, providing a strong legal argument supported by relevant case law.

Predictive Legal Analytics

Scenario: A law firm is assessing the likelihood of success in a potential litigation case and needs to make an informed decision about whether to proceed.

Traditional Approach: The firm would rely on the experience and intuition of its lawyers, without access to comprehensive data on similar cases.

Modern Approach: The firm uses a legal analytics tool like Lex Machina to analyze past case outcomes, identifying factors that contribute to success and estimating the likelihood of winning the case.

Outcome: The firm makes a data-driven decision to proceed with the case, confident in its assessment of the potential risks and rewards.

Contract Analysis

Scenario: A company needs to review a large number of contracts to identify common clauses and potential risks.

Traditional Approach: The legal team would manually review each contract, a time-consuming and labor-intensive process.

Modern Approach: Using a contract analysis tool like Kira Systems, the team can automatically identify common clauses and highlight potential risks across all contracts.

Outcome: The company completes its contract review more quickly and efficiently, ensuring that all potential risks are identified and addressed.

Legal Risk Management

Scenario: A corporation needs to identify and mitigate legal risks related to compliance with new regulations.

Traditional Approach: The legal team would manually review regulations and company policies, a process that could miss important details.

Modern Approach: The corporation uses legal analytics to analyze compliance data, identify gaps, and generate reports on potential risks.

Outcome: The corporation is able to proactively address compliance issues, reducing the risk of legal penalties and ensuring adherence to regulations.

Benefits of Legal Research and Analytics

Efficiency

Digital tools and analytics significantly reduce the time and effort required for legal research and analysis, allowing legal professionals to focus on higher-value tasks.

Accuracy

Advanced search functionalities and data analysis techniques improve the accuracy of legal research, ensuring that relevant information is identified and considered.

Data-Driven Decision Making

Legal analytics provides insights that support data-driven decision-making, helping legal professionals anticipate outcomes and develop effective strategies.

Competitive Advantage

By leveraging advanced legal research and analytics tools, legal professionals can gain a competitive advantage, providing better service to their clients and achieving better outcomes.

Ethical Considerations in Legal Research and Analytics

Data Privacy

Legal professionals must ensure that they comply with data privacy regulations, such as the General Data Protection Regulation (GDPR), when collecting and analyzing data.

Example: A law firm uses data redaction tools to remove sensitive personal information from documents before sharing them with external parties.

Bias in Data

It is important to recognize and address potential biases in data analysis to ensure fair and impartial decision-making.

Example: A legal analytics tool is designed to account for potential biases in historical case data, ensuring that predictions and insights are based on objective criteria.

Conclusion

Legal research and analytics are essential skills for modern legal professionals, enabling them to conduct thorough research, analyze data, and make informed decisions. By understanding and utilizing the tools and techniques available, legal professionals can enhance their efficiency, accuracy, and effectiveness, ultimately providing better service to their clients and achieving better outcomes. In the next chapter, we will explore the role of artificial intelligence in legal practice and how it is transforming the legal industry.

BOOSTING EFFICIENCY IN LAW: LEVERAGING TECHNOLOGY FOR BETTER RESULTS

Introduction to Process Efficiency in Legal Tech

Welcome to the world of process efficiency in Legal Tech! Process efficiency refers to the implementation of solutions that enhance existing practices, streamline routine tasks, and improve overall productivity within legal operations. By leveraging advanced technologies, legal professionals can optimize their workflows, reduce costs, and deliver better services to clients. In this chapter, we will explore the concept of process efficiency in the context of Legal Tech, detailing its key elements and providing practical examples of how these solutions are applied in real-world scenarios. This guide is designed to be easy to understand for beginners while offering in-depth insights for experienced practitioners.

Understanding Process Efficiency

Process efficiency in the legal field involves adopting tools and technologies that simplify and automate tasks, particularly those that are repetitive or time-consuming. The goal is to improve the speed, accuracy, and cost-effectiveness of legal services. This can include everything from automating document generation to managing compliance requirements and intellectual property.

Key Elements of Process Efficiency

Process efficiency in Legal Tech encompasses several key elements, each contributing to the overall improvement of legal operations:

1. **Incorporation Management**
2. **Compliance Management**
3. **Intellectual Property (IP) Management**
4. **Contract Management**
5. **Document Management**
6. **Workflow Automation**
7. **Due Diligence and Risk Analysis**

We will explore each of these elements in detail, highlighting how they enhance process efficiency and providing examples of their application.

Incorporation Management

Overview

Incorporation management solutions assist startups and businesses in efficiently handling their regulatory responsibilities through automated online systems. These tools simplify the process of company registration and other related services, ensuring compliance with legal requirements.

Example: A new tech startup uses an incorporation management platform to register their company, file necessary documents, and obtain legal permits without the need for extensive manual paperwork.

Illustration:

- **Tool**: LegalZoom Business Formation
- **Usage**: The startup founder inputs required information into the platform, which automatically generates and files the necessary documents with the appropriate government agencies.

Compliance Management

Overview

Compliance management tools enable legal professionals to file, track, and monitor compliance requirements. These solutions provide timely updates on regulatory changes and help ensure that businesses remain compliant with relevant laws and regulations.

Example: A financial firm uses a compliance management system to monitor changes in financial regulations and ensure that their practices align with the latest legal requirements.

Illustration:

- **Tool**: Compliance360
- **Usage**: The system tracks regulatory updates, notifies the firm of changes, and provides tools for documenting compliance activities and generating reports.

Intellectual Property (IP) Management

Overview

IP management solutions facilitate the registration and long-term management of intellectual property rights, including patents, trademarks, and copyrights. These tools also offer protection against IP threats and help manage IP portfolios.

Example: A pharmaceutical company uses an IP management platform to register new drug patents, track expiration dates, and monitor for potential infringements.

Illustration:

- **Tool**: Anaqua
- **Usage**: The company inputs patent details into the system, which then tracks registration status, monitors potential infringements, and alerts the company to upcoming renewal dates.

Contract Management

Overview

Contract management solutions automate the entire lifecycle of a contract, from creation to execution. These tools allow legal professionals to create, customize, and track contracts efficiently, ensuring that all parties meet their obligations.

Example: A real estate firm uses a contract management platform to generate lease agreements, track contract milestones, and ensure timely renewals.

Illustration:

- **Tool**: DocuSign CLM
- **Usage**: The firm uploads contract templates into the platform, which then automates the generation and tracking of lease agreements, providing alerts for upcoming renewals and compliance checks.

Document Management

Overview

Document management systems allow users to create, store, and share legal documents securely. These tools help organize and manage legal documents, ensuring that they are easily accessible and compliant with data security standards.

Example: A law firm uses a document management system to store client contracts, legal briefs, and case files, making them accessible to authorized personnel from any location.

Illustration:

- **Tool**: NetDocuments
- **Usage**: The firm uploads documents to the platform, which provides secure storage, version control, and access management features, ensuring that documents are easily accessible and secure.

Workflow Automation

Overview

Workflow automation involves using technology to automate repetitive tasks, such as data entry, document review, and legal research. This helps reduce the time and effort required to complete these tasks, freeing up legal professionals to focus on more strategic activities.

Example: A corporate legal department uses workflow automation tools to automate the review and approval of standard contracts, reducing the time spent on manual reviews.

Illustration:

- **Tool**: UiPath
- **Usage**: The legal department sets up automation workflows that automatically review contracts for standard clauses and flag any deviations for further review by legal staff.

Due Diligence and Risk Analysis

Overview

Due diligence and risk analysis tools enable legal professionals to conduct thorough checks and analyses of financial, litigation, and compliance records. These tools help identify potential risks and ensure that businesses are making informed decisions.

Example: An investment firm uses a due diligence platform to analyze potential acquisition targets, assessing financial health, legal risks, and compliance issues.

Illustration:

- **Tool**: Kira Systems
- **Usage**: The firm inputs financial and legal documents into the platform, which uses AI to analyze the data and identify potential risks and opportunities.

Practical Examples of Process Efficiency in Action

Example 1: Automating Company Formation

Scenario: An entrepreneur wants to start a new business and needs to register the company and obtain necessary permits.

Traditional Approach: The entrepreneur would need to manually complete and file numerous forms with various government agencies, a process that could take weeks.

Process Efficiency Solution: The entrepreneur uses an incorporation management platform like LegalZoom to automate the company formation process, completing all necessary filings and obtaining permits online.

Outcome: The company is registered and operational in a fraction of the time, allowing the entrepreneur to focus on building the business.

Example 2: Streamlining Compliance Monitoring

Scenario: A healthcare provider needs to ensure compliance with ever-changing regulations and monitor ongoing compliance activities.

Traditional Approach: The provider would manually track regulatory changes and compliance activities, which could lead to missed updates and non-compliance risks.

Process Efficiency Solution: The provider uses a compliance management tool like Compliance360 to automate the tracking of regulatory changes and manage compliance activities.

Outcome: The provider stays up-to-date with regulatory changes and ensures ongoing compliance, reducing the risk of penalties and enhancing operational efficiency.

Example 3: Managing Intellectual Property Portfolios

Scenario: A tech company needs to manage a large portfolio of patents and monitor for potential infringements.

Traditional Approach: The company would manually track patent statuses and monitor for potential infringements, a time-consuming and labor-intensive process.

Process Efficiency Solution: The company uses an IP management platform like Anaqua to automate the tracking of patent statuses and monitor for potential infringements.

Outcome: The company efficiently manages its IP portfolio, ensuring timely renewals and protecting against potential infringements, ultimately safeguarding its intellectual property assets.

Example 4: Automating Contract Lifecycle Management

Scenario: A large corporation needs to manage hundreds of contracts with suppliers, customers, and partners.

Traditional Approach: The corporation would manually draft, review, and manage each contract, a process that could lead to delays and missed deadlines.

Process Efficiency Solution: The corporation uses a contract management platform like DocuSign CLM to automate the creation, review, and management of contracts.

Outcome: The corporation streamlines its contract management processes, ensuring that contracts are created and managed efficiently, reducing delays and improving compliance.

Benefits of Process Efficiency

Time Savings

Automating repetitive tasks and streamlining workflows significantly reduces the time required to complete legal processes, allowing legal professionals to focus on higher-value activities.

Cost Reduction

By improving efficiency and reducing the need for manual labor, process efficiency solutions help lower operational costs, making legal services more affordable and accessible.

Improved Accuracy

Automation minimizes the risk of human error, ensuring that legal documents and processes are accurate and compliant with relevant laws and regulations.

Enhanced Productivity

Process efficiency tools enable legal professionals to handle larger volumes of work more effectively, improving overall productivity and client satisfaction.

Conclusion

Process efficiency is a critical aspect of modern legal practice, providing tools and technologies that enhance the speed, accuracy, and cost-effectiveness of legal services. By understanding and implementing these solutions, legal professionals can improve their workflows, reduce costs, and deliver better services to their clients. In the next chapter, we will explore the role of artificial intelligence in legal practice and how it is transforming the legal industry.

MASTERING CONTRACT MANAGEMENT: ESSENTIAL STRATEGIES AND TOOLS

Introduction to Contract Management

Contract management is a crucial aspect of modern legal practice and business operations, involving the creation, negotiation, execution, and monitoring of legal agreements. Effective contract management ensures that all parties meet their obligations and helps mitigate risks associated with non-compliance and disputes. In this chapter, we will explore the fundamentals of contract management, the essential features of contract management software, and practical examples of how these tools are used in real-world scenarios. This guide aims to provide a comprehensive overview of contract management for beginners, using simple language and clear examples to facilitate learning and understanding.

Understanding Contract Management

What is Contract Management?

Contract management refers to the process of managing contracts from their initial creation to their eventual execution and renewal. This includes drafting contracts, negotiating terms, tracking key milestones, and ensuring compliance with legal and regulatory requirements.

Example: A company needs to manage contracts with multiple suppliers. Effective contract management ensures that all agreements are clear, obligations are met, and any risks are identified and addressed in a timely manner.

The Importance of Contract Management

Effective contract management helps organizations avoid legal disputes, reduce costs, and improve relationships with clients and partners. It ensures that contracts are completed on time, terms are enforced, and obligations are fulfilled.

Example: A real estate firm that manages hundreds of lease agreements uses contract management to track renewal dates, ensuring that tenants are notified well in advance and leases are renewed without disruption.

Key Features of Contract Management Software

Contract management software provides tools that simplify and automate the contract lifecycle. Here are some essential features to look for in a contract management solution:

1. Contract Repository

A centralized repository allows for the secure storage and easy retrieval of contract documents. It should support various document types and provide robust search capabilities.

Example: A law firm uses a contract management system with a centralized repository to store and organize all client contracts, making it easy for attorneys to access and review agreements as needed.

Illustration:

- **Tool**: ContractWorks
- **Usage**: The firm uploads contracts to the system, where they are indexed and stored securely, allowing quick access and retrieval through a simple search interface.

2. Customizable Templates

Customizable templates enable users to create contracts that meet specific requirements. These templates should be user-friendly and easy to modify.

Example: A tech company uses contract management software to create standardized employment contracts by filling out a template, ensuring consistency across all agreements.

Illustration:

- **Tool**: Concord
- **Usage**: The company creates and saves templates for different contract types, which can be quickly customized for new employees or clients.

3. Collaboration and Sharing

Effective contract management software should facilitate easy collaboration and sharing of contracts, both internally and externally. This includes features for real-time editing, comments, and feedback.

Example: A multinational corporation uses a contract management platform to collaborate on contracts with legal teams in different countries, ensuring that all stakeholders can review and approve documents simultaneously.

Illustration:

- **Tool**: PandaDoc
- **Usage**: Team members can edit and comment on contract drafts in real time, with changes tracked and approvals managed within the platform.

4. Notification System

A customizable notification system alerts users to important contract milestones, such as expiration or renewal dates, ensuring that critical deadlines are not missed.

Example: An insurance company uses contract management software to receive alerts about policy renewal dates, ensuring timely follow-ups with clients.

Illustration:

- **Tool**: Agiloft
- **Usage**: The system sends automated notifications to the relevant team members about upcoming contract renewals or required actions, helping them stay on top of key deadlines.

5. Compliance and Security

The software must comply with relevant legal and regulatory requirements and provide robust security features to protect sensitive contract information.

Example: A healthcare provider uses contract management software that complies with data protection regulations, ensuring that patient data in contracts is securely stored and managed.

Illustration:

- **Tool**: ContractSafe
- **Usage**: The platform offers encryption and access controls, ensuring that only authorized personnel can access or modify sensitive contract information.

Practical Examples of Contract Management in Action

Example 1: Automating Contract Creation

Scenario: A small business needs to create multiple vendor contracts quickly and accurately.

Traditional Approach: The business owner would manually draft each contract, a process that could be time-consuming and prone to errors.

Contract Management Solution: The business uses contract management software like Concord to create contracts using pre-built templates, which can be customized with specific details.

Outcome: The business efficiently generates accurate contracts, reducing the time spent on manual drafting and minimizing the risk of errors.

Example 2: Streamlining Contract Negotiation

Scenario: A law firm needs to negotiate a complex contract with a client and several external stakeholders.

Traditional Approach: The firm would send drafts back and forth via email, which could lead to confusion and delays.

Contract Management Solution: The firm uses PandaDoc to collaborate on contract drafts in real time, allowing all parties to review, comment, and approve changes simultaneously.

Outcome: The negotiation process is streamlined, reducing delays and ensuring that all stakeholders have access to the latest contract version.

Example 3: Ensuring Compliance with Contract Terms

Scenario: A manufacturing company needs to ensure compliance with supplier contracts to avoid penalties for non-compliance.

Traditional Approach: The company would manually track contract terms and compliance requirements, which could lead to missed obligations and penalties.

Contract Management Solution: The company uses Agiloft to track contract terms and compliance requirements, with automated alerts for upcoming deadlines and compliance checks.

Outcome: The company stays compliant with contract terms, avoiding penalties and maintaining good relationships with suppliers.

Example 4: Managing Contract Renewals

Scenario: A real estate firm needs to manage the renewal of hundreds of lease agreements.

Traditional Approach: The firm would manually track renewal dates, leading to the risk of missed deadlines and disruptions in lease agreements.

Contract Management Solution: The firm uses ContractSafe to track lease agreement terms and send automated notifications about upcoming renewals.

Outcome: The firm efficiently manages lease renewals, ensuring that agreements are renewed on time and reducing the risk of disruptions.

Benefits of Contract Management

Efficiency

Contract management software streamlines the contract lifecycle, from creation to execution, reducing the time and effort required to manage contracts manually.

Accuracy

Automation minimizes the risk of human error, ensuring that contracts are accurate and compliant with relevant legal and regulatory requirements.

Compliance

Contract management tools help organizations stay compliant with legal and regulatory requirements, reducing the risk of penalties and legal disputes.

Cost Savings

By improving efficiency and reducing the need for manual labor, contract management software helps lower operational costs and improves the bottom line.

Improved Relationships

Effective contract management helps organizations maintain good relationships with clients, partners, and suppliers by ensuring that obligations are met and disputes are minimized.

Selecting the Right Contract Management Tool

Key Considerations

When selecting a contract management tool, consider the following factors:

- **Ease of Use**: The software should be user-friendly and easy to navigate.
- **Customization**: Look for tools that offer customizable templates and features to meet your specific needs.
- **Integration**: Ensure the software integrates with other tools and systems you use, such as CRM and accounting software.

- **Security**: Choose a tool that provides robust security features to protect sensitive contract information.
- **Support**: Opt for software that offers good customer support and training resources.

Popular Contract Management Tools

Here are some popular contract management tools to consider:

- **ContractWorks**: Known for its ease of use and robust security features.
- **Concord**: Offers customizable templates and collaboration tools.
- **PandaDoc**: Provides real-time collaboration and e-signature capabilities.
- **Agiloft**: Features comprehensive compliance tracking and automated notifications.
- **ContractSafe**: Known for its secure document storage and easy retrieval features.

Conclusion

Contract management is an essential component of legal and business operations, helping organizations create, manage, and comply with their agreements efficiently and effectively. By leveraging contract management software, legal professionals can streamline their workflows, reduce risks, and improve their overall contract management processes. In the next chapter, we will explore the role of artificial intelligence in contract management and how it is transforming the way contracts are handled.

WORKFLOW AUTOMATION, DOCUMENT AUTOMATION, AND DUE DILIGENCE: LEGAL TECH SOLUTIONS

Introduction

Welcome to the comprehensive guide on Workflow Automation, Document Automation, and Due Diligence within the realm of Legal Tech. These processes are essential for enhancing efficiency, reducing manual workloads, and ensuring thorough analysis and compliance in legal operations. In this chapter, we will explore the basics of each topic, the technologies involved, and practical examples to illustrate their application. This guide is tailored for beginners, with straightforward explanations and real-world examples to help you grasp these critical aspects of modern legal practice.

Workflow Automation

What is Workflow Automation?

Workflow automation involves using technology to streamline and automate repetitive tasks and processes. This helps legal professionals save time, reduce errors, and increase efficiency by allowing them to focus on more strategic activities.

Example: A law firm uses workflow automation to manage client intake processes, automatically assigning tasks and sending notifications to relevant team members, ensuring a smooth and timely onboarding of new clients.

Key Features of Workflow Automation Tools

1. **Task Management**: Automate the assignment and tracking of tasks to ensure deadlines are met.
2. **Notifications and Alerts**: Automatically notify users of upcoming deadlines and important events.
3. **Integration with Other Tools**: Seamlessly integrate with other software to streamline processes across platforms.
4. **Drag-and-Drop Workflow Creation**: Easily design workflows with a user-friendly interface.
5. **Form Creation and Collaboration**: Create forms for data collection and facilitate collaboration among team members.

Illustration:

- **Tool**: Asana
- **Usage**: A legal team uses Asana to track project progress, assign tasks, and collaborate on case documents, all in one platform.

Practical Example of Workflow Automation

Scenario: A legal department in a large corporation needs to streamline the process of managing compliance with regulatory changes.

Traditional Approach: The department would manually track changes, assign tasks, and follow up on compliance activities, a process prone to delays and errors.

Workflow Automation Solution: The department uses a tool like Monday.com to automate task assignments and notifications. When a regulatory change is detected, the system automatically assigns compliance tasks to the relevant team members and sends reminders as deadlines approach.

Outcome: The compliance process becomes more efficient, with fewer errors and delays, ensuring that the company stays compliant with legal requirements.

Document Automation

What is Document Automation?

Document automation refers to the use of software to create, manage, and store legal documents automatically. This reduces the need for manual drafting and ensures consistency and accuracy across all documents.

Example: A law firm uses document automation to generate standard legal contracts by filling out a template with specific client information, ensuring all contracts are compliant and up-to-date.

Key Features of Document Automation Tools

1. **Template Management**: Create and store reusable templates for various document types.
2. **Automated Document Generation**: Generate documents by populating templates with relevant data.
3. **Version Control**: Keep track of document versions and changes to maintain a clear audit trail.
4. **Secure Storage and Sharing**: Store documents securely and share them with authorized users.

5. **Integration with Other Systems**: Integrate with other legal and business systems to streamline document workflows.

Illustration:

- **Tool**: NetDocuments
- **Usage**: A law firm uses NetDocuments to create, manage, and store legal documents securely, allowing lawyers to collaborate and access documents from anywhere.

Practical Example of Document Automation

Scenario: A real estate firm needs to create and manage lease agreements for multiple properties.

Traditional Approach: The firm would manually draft each lease agreement, a time-consuming process that could lead to inconsistencies and errors.

Document Automation Solution: The firm uses a document automation tool like Actionstep to generate lease agreements from a template, filling in specific details for each property.

Outcome: The firm saves time and ensures that all lease agreements are consistent and accurate, reducing the risk of legal issues and improving efficiency.

Due Diligence

What is Due Diligence?

Due diligence is the process of thoroughly investigating and evaluating the details of a potential business transaction or investment to identify and mitigate risks. This typically involves examining financial records, legal documents, contracts, and other relevant information.

Example: An investment firm conducts due diligence on a startup to assess its financial health, legal compliance, and potential risks before making an investment.

Key Features of Due Diligence Tools

1. **Document Review and Analysis**: Tools for reviewing and analyzing large volumes of documents to identify key information and potential risks.

2. **Data Collection and Organization**: Collect and organize data from various sources to facilitate thorough analysis.

3. **Risk Assessment and Reporting**: Identify risks and generate reports to provide a comprehensive overview of findings.
4. **Collaboration and Sharing**: Facilitate collaboration among team members and stakeholders, and securely share information.
5. **Integration with Other Systems**: Integrate with other tools for a seamless due diligence process.

Illustration:
- **Tool**: Kira Systems
- **Usage**: A legal team uses Kira Systems to review contracts and identify key clauses and potential issues, speeding up the due diligence process and improving accuracy.

Practical Example of Due Diligence

Scenario: A corporation is considering acquiring a smaller company and needs to conduct due diligence to assess potential risks and liabilities.

Traditional Approach: The corporation would manually review all the smaller company's documents, a process that could take weeks and might miss important details.

Due Diligence Solution: The corporation uses a virtual data room like Ansarada to collect and review all relevant documents, and a tool like Relativity to analyze the data and identify key risks.

Outcome: The due diligence process is completed more quickly and thoroughly, providing a clear picture of the smaller company's financial health and potential risks, allowing the corporation to make an informed decision.

Benefits of Workflow Automation, Document Automation, and Due Diligence

Increased Efficiency

Automation reduces the time and effort required for repetitive tasks, allowing legal professionals to focus on higher-value activities.

Improved Accuracy

Automated systems minimize the risk of human error, ensuring that tasks are completed accurately and consistently.

Cost Savings

By streamlining processes and reducing manual labor, automation helps lower operational costs and improve profitability.

Enhanced Collaboration

Automation tools facilitate collaboration among team members and stakeholders, improving communication and workflow.

Better Risk Management

Due diligence tools help identify potential risks early, allowing organizations to address them proactively and avoid costly legal issues.

Choosing the Right Tools

Key Considerations

When selecting automation and due diligence tools, consider the following factors:

- **Ease of Use**: The tools should be user-friendly and easy to integrate into existing workflows.
- **Customization**: Look for tools that can be customized to meet your specific needs and requirements.
- **Integration**: Ensure that the tools integrate seamlessly with other systems and software you use.
- **Security**: Choose tools that provide robust security features to protect sensitive information.
- **Support**: Opt for vendors that offer good customer support and training resources.

Popular Tools

Here are some popular tools for workflow automation, document automation, and due diligence:

- **Workflow Automation**: Asana, Trello, Monday.com, Legal Tracker
- **Document Automation**: NetDocuments, iManage, Actionstep, ContractWorks
- **Due Diligence**: Kira Systems, Ansarada, Relativity, Intralinks

Conclusion

Workflow automation, document automation, and due diligence are critical components of modern legal practice, offering tools and technologies that enhance efficiency, reduce risks, and improve overall operations. By understanding and implementing these solutions, legal professionals can streamline their workflows, ensure compliance, and make more informed decisions. In the next chapter, we will explore the role of artificial intelligence in legal practice and how it is transforming the legal industry.

THE LEGAL TECH IMPLEMENTATION FRAMEWORK: KEY STEPS FOR SUCCESS

Introduction to Legal Tech Implementation

Implementing Legal Tech in any organization can significantly enhance efficiency, streamline workflows, and improve overall productivity. However, successful implementation requires a well-thought-out framework that considers the interplay between technology, people, and organizational culture. This chapter will guide you through the key steps of a Legal Tech implementation framework, offering practical advice and real-world examples to help you understand and apply these principles effectively. This guide is designed to be accessible for beginners, using clear language and examples to facilitate learning and application.

Overview of the Implementation Framework

To effectively implement Legal Tech, it is crucial to address not only the technology itself but also the individuals who will use it and the organization's goals and culture. A structured approach helps maximize the benefits of Legal Tech while minimizing potential challenges.

Key Steps in the Implementation Framework

1. Identify the Problem
2. Evaluate Requirements
3. Determine the Technology Solution
4. Plan for Implementation
5. Communicate with Stakeholders
6. Create a Business Case
7. Training and Education
8. Integration with Existing Systems
9. Onboarding
10. Monitor and Evaluate
11. Continuous Improvement

Step-by-Step Implementation Guide

Step 1: Identify the Problem

Determine the specific pain points and inefficiencies in your legal department that need to be addressed through Legal Tech. Clearly define the challenges and objectives you aim to achieve through the optimization process.

Example: A law firm struggles with the manual handling of large volumes of client contracts, leading to delays and errors. The objective is to automate contract management to improve accuracy and efficiency.

Step 2: Evaluate Requirements

Consider financial constraints and evaluate the potential return on investment (ROI). Assess if your organization has a culture that supports change and innovation. Identify the essential features and functionalities needed in the Legal Tech solution.

Example: The law firm evaluates its budget and determines that the ROI for an automated contract management system would be positive due to time savings and reduced error rates.

Step 3: Determine the Technology Solution

Research different Legal Tech options available in the market and assess their suitability for your specific needs. Look for tools that offer the necessary features and align with your organizational goals.

Example: The law firm reviews various contract management systems, such as ContractSafe and DocuSign, to find a solution that fits its requirements and budget.

Step 4: Plan for Implementation

Create a detailed plan for implementing the chosen technology solution. The plan should include a timeline, budget, and milestones. Consider the resources required and potential risks involved in the implementation process.

Example: The law firm develops a project plan that includes setting up the contract management system, training staff, and integrating the system with existing workflows over a three-month period.

Step 5: Communicate with Stakeholders

Communicate with all stakeholders involved in the implementation process, including lawyers, support staff, and clients. Explain why the technology is being implemented, how it will benefit the organization, and how it will be used.

Example: The law firm holds meetings with its legal team and administrative staff to discuss the benefits of the new contract management system and how it will streamline their work processes.

Step 6: Create a Business Case

Develop a business case that includes the proposed solution, estimated costs, expected economic benefits, potential risks, and project evaluation metrics. Use this business case to justify the investment in Legal Tech.

Example: The law firm prepares a business case showing that the contract management system will reduce contract processing time by 50%, leading to significant cost savings and improved client satisfaction.

Step 7: Training and Education

Provide comprehensive training for all users on how to use the technology and understand its capabilities. Ensure that training covers all aspects of the tool and is tailored to the needs of different user groups.

Example: The law firm arranges training sessions for its staff on how to use the new contract management system, including hands-on practice and support materials.

Step 8: Integration with Existing Systems

Ensure that the technology solution can be integrated with your existing systems. Plan and execute the integration carefully to avoid disruptions and ensure smooth workflow transitions.

Example: The law firm integrates the contract management system with its existing document management and email systems to enable seamless document sharing and collaboration.

Step 9: Onboarding

Provide proper onboarding for key users and regular users. Implement a phased approach to training and usage, allowing time for users to gain confidence and become proficient with the new technology.

Example: The law firm designates key users to receive advanced training on the contract management system. These key users then assist in training other staff members and provide ongoing support.

Step 10: Monitor and Evaluate

After implementation, monitor the use of the technology and evaluate its effectiveness. Identify areas for improvement and ensure that the technology is being used to its full potential.

Example: The law firm regularly reviews the performance of the contract management system, gathering feedback from users and making adjustments to improve efficiency and user satisfaction.

Step 11: Continuous Improvement

Continuously assess and improve the technology solution. Regularly review its effectiveness and seek feedback from users to identify opportunities for improvement. Ensure that the technology continues to meet the organization's needs.

Example: The law firm conducts periodic assessments of the contract management system, implementing updates and enhancements based on user feedback to keep the system up-to-date and effective.

Practical Examples of Legal Tech Implementation

Example 1: Implementing a Document Management System

Scenario: A corporate legal department needs to improve the management of legal documents, which are currently scattered across multiple systems and locations.

Solution: The department implements a document management system like NetDocuments to centralize document storage, improve search capabilities, and enhance collaboration.

Outcome: The department reduces the time spent searching for documents, improves document security, and enhances collaboration among team members.

Example 2: Automating Workflow Processes

Scenario: A law firm needs to streamline the process of managing client intake and case assignment.

Solution: The firm uses a workflow automation tool like Trello to automate client intake processes, assign tasks, and track case progress.

Outcome: The firm improves the efficiency of its client intake process, reduces manual errors, and ensures timely case assignments.

Example 3: Enhancing Due Diligence with Technology

Scenario: An investment firm needs to conduct thorough due diligence on potential acquisition targets.

Solution: The firm uses a due diligence platform like Kira Systems to analyze contracts and identify key risks and opportunities.

Outcome: The firm completes the due diligence process more quickly and accurately, allowing for informed investment decisions.

Tips for Smoother Implementation

1. **Build Internal Champions**: Identify innovators and early adopters who can advocate for the new technology and encourage others to embrace it.
2. **Communicate the Benefits**: Clearly explain how the technology will benefit the organization and its users in the long run.
3. **Integrate Technology into Workflows**: Work the new technology into existing workflows gradually to facilitate adoption and integration.
4. **Leverage Vendor Support**: Utilize vendor training and support services to ensure users are well-educated on the new tool.
5. **Celebrate Success**: Recognize and celebrate the successes achieved with the new technology to motivate continued use and improvement.

Conclusion

Implementing Legal Tech requires a thoughtful and structured approach that considers the interaction of technology, people, and the organization. By following the outlined framework, legal professionals can ensure a smooth and successful adoption of Legal Tech solutions, leading to improved efficiency, reduced costs, and better overall performance. In the next chapter, we will explore the role of artificial intelligence in legal practice and how it is transforming the legal industry.

THE VALUE OF LEGAL TECH: MEASURING RETURN ON INVESTMENT (ROI)

Introduction to Calculating ROI for Legal Technology

Calculating the return on investment (ROI) for legal technology is crucial for demonstrating its value to stakeholders and ensuring that the investment aligns with organizational goals. ROI provides a quantitative measure of the financial benefits gained from an investment relative to its cost, helping legal professionals make informed decisions about adopting new technologies. In this chapter, we will explore the concept of ROI, the factors to consider when calculating it, and practical examples to illustrate how to demonstrate the value of legal technology investments effectively.

Understanding Return on Investment (ROI)

What is ROI?

ROI stands for Return on Investment. It is a financial metric used to evaluate the efficiency of an investment by comparing the gains from the investment to its cost. The formula for calculating ROI is:

$$ROI = \frac{(\text{Total Benefit of Investment} - \text{Cost of Investment})}{\text{Cost of Investment}}$$

Example: If a law firm invests $10,000 in a new legal research tool and saves $15,000 in reduced labor costs over a year, the ROI would be calculated as follows:

$$ROI = \frac{(15,000 - 10,000)}{10,000} = 0.5 \text{ or } 50\%$$

This means the firm gained a 50% return on their investment.

Key Factors for Calculating ROI

1. Define Objectives and Goals

Identify the specific goals you want to achieve with the legal technology, such as reducing costs, improving efficiency, or enhancing compliance. Clearly defining these objectives helps measure the benefits accurately.

Example: A corporate legal department aims to reduce the time spent on contract review by 30% through the use of an AI-powered document review tool.

2. Assess Costs and Savings

Consider both the direct costs (e.g., software purchase, implementation) and indirect costs (e.g., training, maintenance). Evaluate the potential savings, such as reduced labor costs, increased productivity, and improved compliance.

Example: The department evaluates the cost of the AI tool, including the purchase price and training costs, and compares it to the savings in labor costs from reduced document review time.

3. Measure Efficiency Gains

Determine how the technology will improve efficiency by reducing the time and resources required to complete tasks. Consider metrics like time savings, error reduction, and increased task completion rates.

Example: The AI tool reduces the time required for document review from 5 hours to 2 hours per contract, resulting in significant time savings.

4. Consider Convenience and Scalability

Evaluate how easy it is to implement the technology and whether it can scale with the organization's needs. Assess if the technology disrupts current processes or integrates seamlessly.

Example: The department finds that the AI tool is easy to integrate with their existing document management system and can handle increasing volumes of documents as the organization grows.

5. Identify Key Performance Indicators (KPIs)

Establish KPIs to measure the impact of the technology before and after implementation. KPIs might include the number of contracts processed, time to contract approval, or the percentage of errors detected.

Example: The department sets KPIs to measure the number of contracts reviewed per week and the time taken to complete each review before and after using the AI tool.

Calculating ROI: Practical Examples

Example 1: ROI for Contract Management System

Scenario: A legal department implements a contract management system to streamline the contract approval process.

Costs: The system costs $20,000 for software and $5,000 for training and implementation.

Savings: The system reduces contract processing time by 50%, resulting in annual labor savings of $30,000.

ROI Calculation:

$$ROI = \frac{(30,000 - 25,000)}{25,000} = 0.2 \text{ or } 20\%$$

Outcome: The legal department achieves a 20% return on their investment, demonstrating the value of the contract management system.

Example 2: ROI for E-Discovery Tool

Scenario: A law firm adopts an e-discovery tool to manage large volumes of electronic data for litigation cases.

Costs: The tool costs $50,000 per year, including software, training, and maintenance.

Savings: The tool saves $75,000 per year in labor costs by automating the data review process and reducing the time required for manual review.

ROI Calculation:

$$ROI = \frac{(75,000 - 50,000)}{50,000} = 0.5 \text{ or } 50\%$$

Outcome: The law firm gains a 50% return on their investment, justifying the expenditure on the e-discovery tool.

Example 3: ROI for Document Automation Software

Scenario: A corporate legal team implements document automation software to create and manage legal documents.

Costs: The software costs $15,000 per year, including the subscription fee and training.

Savings: The software reduces the time spent on document creation by 40%, resulting in annual savings of $20,000 in labor costs.

ROI Calculation:

$$ROI = \frac{(20,000 - 15,000)}{15,000} = 0.33 \text{ or } 33\%$$

Outcome: The corporate legal team achieves a 33% return on their investment, highlighting the efficiency and cost savings provided by the document automation software.

Simplified ROI Calculation Method

Back-of-the-Envelope Method

A quick way to estimate ROI involves comparing the cost and benefits of the new technology with a simplified approach:

1. **Identify Process Changes**: Outline the old and new processes.
2. **Estimate Time and Cost Savings**: Compare the time and cost of completing tasks before and after implementation.
3. **Calculate ROI**: Use the simplified formula to estimate ROI based on time and cost savings.

Example: A legal team shifts from a manual contract approval process to a digital process using e-signature software.

Old Process: Print and sign contracts, send for additional signatures, scan, and store (total time: 5 hours).

New Process: Upload contracts to a digital platform, collect e-signatures, and store online (total time: 2 hours).

Time Savings: 3 hours per contract.

Cost Savings: Reduced labor costs for each contract processed (e.g., $150 savings per contract).

Simplified ROI Calculation:

$$\text{ROI} = \frac{(\text{Total Cost Savings} - \text{Cost of Technology})}{\text{Cost of Technology}}$$

Outcome: If the cost of the e-signature software is $10,000 per year and it saves $20,000 in labor costs, the ROI would be 100%.

Key Performance Indicators (KPIs)

Importance of KPIs

KPIs are crucial for measuring the effectiveness of legal technology and assessing its impact on the organization. They help track progress, identify areas for improvement, and demonstrate the value of the technology to stakeholders.

Examples of KPIs

- **Number of Documents Processed**: Measure the volume of documents handled before and after implementation.
- **Time to Task Completion**: Track the time required to complete specific tasks, such as contract review or document creation.
- **Error Rate Reduction**: Monitor the decrease in errors or discrepancies in document processing.
- **Cost Savings**: Calculate the financial savings achieved through reduced labor costs and increased efficiency.
- **User Adoption Rate**: Measure the percentage of users who have adopted the new technology and are actively using it.

Example: A legal team tracks the number of contracts processed and the time taken to complete each review before and after implementing an AI document review tool. The KPIs show a 50% increase in the number of contracts reviewed per week and a 30% reduction in review time.

Demonstrating the Value to Stakeholders

Communicate Benefits Clearly

Clearly communicate the benefits of the legal technology to stakeholders, including the financial savings, efficiency gains, and improved compliance. Use quantifiable metrics and KPIs to support your case.

Example: A law firm presents the ROI and KPIs for their new e-discovery tool to senior management, highlighting the cost savings and increased productivity.

Use Real-World Examples

Provide real-world examples and case studies to demonstrate how the technology has benefited other organizations. Highlight the tangible outcomes and success stories to build a compelling case.

Example: The law firm shares a case study of another firm that successfully implemented the same e-discovery tool, resulting in significant cost savings and improved case outcomes.

Address Potential Concerns

Anticipate and address any potential concerns or objections from stakeholders, such as the cost of implementation or disruption to existing workflows. Provide solutions and reassurance to alleviate these concerns.

Example: The law firm addresses concerns about the cost of the e-discovery tool by presenting a detailed cost-benefit analysis and a phased implementation plan to minimize disruption.

Conclusion

Calculating and demonstrating the ROI of legal technology is essential for proving its value and justifying the investment. By understanding the factors involved in calculating ROI, establishing relevant KPIs, and effectively communicating the benefits to stakeholders, legal professionals can make informed decisions about adopting new technologies. This chapter provides a comprehensive guide to demonstrating the value of legal technology, making it accessible for beginners and valuable for experienced practitioners.

DIY LEGAL TOOLS: FEATURES, BENEFITS, AND BEST USES

Introduction to DIY Legal Tools

In recent years, the legal landscape has seen a significant shift towards the adoption of DIY (Do It Yourself) legal tools. These tools empower individuals and businesses to manage their legal needs independently, without requiring direct involvement from legal professionals for basic legal tasks. DIY legal tools are designed to simplify legal processes, making them more accessible and affordable for everyone. This chapter will provide a comprehensive overview of DIY legal tools, discussing their key features, benefits, and practical applications with illustrative examples to help you understand how to use them effectively.

What Are DIY Legal Tools?

DIY legal tools are online platforms and software that provide users with the ability to create, manage, and execute legal documents and tasks without the need for a lawyer. They cover a broad range of legal needs, from document creation and electronic signatures to legal consultations and court filings.

Example: A small business owner uses a DIY legal platform to draft a simple contract for a freelance project, eliminating the need to hire a lawyer for basic document creation.

Key Features of DIY Legal Tools

1. Document Drafting

DIY legal tools often include document drafting features, allowing users to create legal documents such as contracts, wills, and leases using pre-made templates that can be customized to meet specific requirements.

Example: A landlord uses a DIY platform to draft a lease agreement by selecting a template and entering details about the rental property and terms of the lease.

Illustration:

- **Tool**: LawDepot
- **Usage:** The landlord selects a lease template, fills in the necessary information, and downloads the completed lease for use with their tenant.

2. E-Signatures and Digital Signatures

These tools provide secure methods for signing and executing legal documents electronically, ensuring that agreements are legally binding and recognized across jurisdictions.

Example: A freelancer uses an e-signature tool to sign a contract with a client, ensuring that the agreement is legally valid and enforceable.

Illustration:

- **Tool**: DocuSign
- **Usage**: The freelancer uploads the contract, sends it to the client for signing, and both parties sign the document electronically.

3. Legal Consultations

Some DIY platforms offer access to legal advice and consultations, allowing users to get professional guidance on their legal issues without the need for a full-time lawyer.

Example: An individual seeking advice on creating a will uses a DIY platform to consult with a lawyer online, receiving guidance on how to structure their will.

Illustration:

- **Tool**: Rocket Lawyer
- **Usage**: The individual schedules an online consultation with a lawyer to discuss their estate planning needs.

4. Online Court Filings

DIY legal tools enable users to file legal documents with courts electronically, simplifying the process of submitting legal paperwork and reducing the time and cost associated with traditional paper filings.

Example: A law firm uses an online filing tool to submit documents for a case, saving time and avoiding the need to physically visit the courthouse.

Illustration:

- **Tool**: One Legal
- **Usage**: The law firm uploads court documents to the platform, which then files them electronically with the appropriate court.

5. Compliance and Registration

These tools help users meet regulatory requirements and complete necessary registrations, such as business formation or trademark applications, through a streamlined online process.

Example: An entrepreneur uses a DIY tool to register a new business with the state, ensuring compliance with all legal requirements without needing to hire a lawyer.

Illustration:

- **Tool**: LegalZoom
- **Usage**: The entrepreneur selects the business type, provides necessary information, and the tool handles the registration process with the state.

Benefits of DIY Legal Tools

Cost-Effectiveness

DIY legal tools provide a cost-effective alternative to hiring lawyers for basic legal tasks, reducing legal expenses and making legal services more accessible to a wider audience.

Example: A startup saves money by using a DIY platform to draft employment contracts, avoiding the higher costs of hiring a lawyer for each document.

Convenience and Accessibility

These tools offer the convenience of handling legal matters online, at any time and from any location, making it easier for users to manage their legal needs.

Example: An individual living in a rural area uses a DIY tool to create a power of attorney document without needing to travel to a law office.

Speed and Efficiency

DIY legal tools streamline the legal process, allowing users to complete legal tasks more quickly and efficiently than traditional methods.

Example: A business owner uses a DIY platform to file a trademark application in a matter of hours, compared to the longer timeline of traditional filing methods.

Empowerment and Control

These tools empower users by giving them control over their legal matters, allowing them to handle tasks independently and gain a better understanding of the legal process.

Example: A homeowner uses a DIY tool to draft a will, gaining confidence in managing their own legal affairs and ensuring their wishes are clearly documented.

Practical Examples of DIY Legal Tools

Example 1: Creating a Simple Contract

Scenario: A freelance graphic designer needs to create a contract for a new client project.

Traditional Approach: The designer would need to hire a lawyer to draft the contract, which could be costly and time-consuming.

DIY Solution: The designer uses a DIY legal tool like LawDepot to select a contract template, customize it with project details, and download the completed contract for signing.

Outcome: The designer creates a professional contract quickly and at a lower cost, ensuring that the terms of the project are clearly outlined and legally binding.

Example 2: Filing for Business Formation

Scenario: An entrepreneur wants to start a new business and needs to register the company with the state.

Traditional Approach: The entrepreneur would need to hire a lawyer to handle the registration process, which could involve multiple meetings and a lengthy timeline.

DIY Solution: The entrepreneur uses a DIY platform like LegalZoom to select the business type, complete the necessary forms, and submit the registration online.

Outcome: The business is registered quickly and efficiently, allowing the entrepreneur to focus on launching and growing their new venture.

Example 3: Executing a Lease Agreement

Scenario: A landlord needs to create and sign a lease agreement with a new tenant.

Traditional Approach: The landlord would need to draft the lease, print multiple copies, and arrange for in-person signing, which could be inconvenient and time-consuming.

DIY Solution: The landlord uses an e-signature tool like DocuSign to upload the lease, send it to the tenant for electronic signing, and store the signed document securely online.

Outcome: The lease agreement is created, signed, and stored quickly and securely, streamlining the rental process and reducing administrative burden.

Example 4: Completing a Will

Scenario: An individual needs to create a will to ensure their estate is distributed according to their wishes.

Traditional Approach: The individual would need to consult with a lawyer to draft the will, which could involve multiple meetings and significant legal fees.

DIY Solution: The individual uses a DIY platform like Rocket Lawyer to select a will template, customize it with their specific instructions, and download the completed will for signing.

Outcome: The individual creates a legally binding will quickly and affordably, ensuring that their estate is managed according to their wishes.

Challenges and Considerations

Legal Complexity

DIY legal tools are best suited for simple legal tasks and may not be appropriate for complex legal issues that require professional legal advice and expertise.

Example: A business dealing with complex litigation may need to hire a lawyer for specialized legal advice, rather than relying solely on DIY tools.

Regulatory Compliance

Users must ensure that the DIY tools they choose comply with relevant legal and regulatory requirements in their jurisdiction.

Example: An individual using a DIY tool to create a will must ensure that the tool is compliant with state-specific estate planning laws to ensure the will is valid.

Security and Confidentiality

DIY tools must provide robust security measures to protect sensitive legal information and ensure confidentiality.

Example: A law firm using an online filing tool must ensure that the platform uses encryption and other security measures to protect client data during transmission and storage.

Limitations of DIY Tools

While DIY tools offer many benefits, they may have limitations in terms of customization and flexibility compared to traditional legal services.

Example: A landlord using a DIY tool to create a lease agreement may find that the template does not fully address specific legal requirements or unique terms needed for their rental property.

Choosing the Right DIY Legal Tools

Key Considerations

When selecting a DIY legal tool, consider the following factors:

- **Ease of Use**: The tool should be user-friendly and easy to navigate.
- **Compliance**: Ensure that the tool complies with relevant legal requirements in your jurisdiction.
- **Security**: Choose a tool that provides robust security features to protect your information.
- **Support**: Look for tools that offer customer support and resources to assist with any issues.
- **Reviews and Recommendations**: Research user reviews and seek recommendations to find reliable and effective tools.

Popular DIY Legal Tools

Here are some popular DIY legal tools to consider:

- **LawDepot**: Offers a wide range of customizable legal document templates.
- **LegalZoom**: Provides tools for business formation, wills, and other legal documents.
- **Rocket Lawyer**: Offers legal document templates, consultations, and advice.
- **DocuSign**: Provides e-signature solutions for securely signing and managing documents.
- **One Legal**: Offers online court filing and document services for legal professionals.

Conclusion

DIY legal tools provide a valuable resource for individuals and businesses to manage their legal needs independently and affordably. By understanding the key features, benefits, and applications of these tools, you can effectively utilize them to handle a variety of legal tasks. In the next chapter, we will explore the role of artificial intelligence in legal practice and how it is transforming the legal industry.

MASTERING DIY LEGAL TOOLS: E-SIGNING, DIGITAL SIGNATURES, AND DOCUMENT DRAFTING

Introduction to DIY Legal Tools

DIY legal tools are becoming increasingly popular due to their convenience, affordability, and ease of use. These tools are particularly useful for handling straightforward legal tasks, such as e-signing documents, drafting simple contracts, and managing basic legal agreements. However, it's essential to understand how and when to use these tools effectively to avoid potential legal pitfalls and ensure that you are making informed decisions. This chapter will guide you through the proper use of DIY tools for e-signing, digital signatures, and document drafting, providing practical examples to help you apply these tools in real-world scenarios.

Understanding DIY Legal Tools

What Are DIY Legal Tools?

DIY legal tools are online platforms and software that enable individuals and businesses to handle their legal needs independently, without the need for professional legal services for routine tasks. These tools include features for document drafting, e-signing, and managing legal documents, making them ideal for simple legal matters.

Example: A small business uses a DIY legal platform to draft employment contracts and obtain e-signatures from new hires, saving time and reducing legal costs.

When to Use DIY Tools

DIY legal tools are most appropriate for straightforward legal tasks that do not require specialized legal advice. Here are some common scenarios where DIY tools are highly effective:

1. Simple Document Drafting

Use DIY tools for drafting standard legal documents that require minimal customization and are not legally complex. These documents include rental agreements, non-disclosure agreements, and basic service contracts.

Example: A freelancer uses a DIY legal tool to draft a standard service contract for a new client, specifying the scope of work and payment terms.

2. E-Signing and Digital Signatures

Use e-signature and digital signature tools for signing documents electronically, ensuring that agreements are legally binding and recognized in multiple jurisdictions.

Example: A real estate agent uses an e-signature tool to sign a lease agreement with a tenant, eliminating the need for physical paperwork and in-person meetings.

3. Managing Routine Legal Tasks

Use DIY tools to manage routine legal tasks such as business formation, trademark registration, and basic compliance filings.

Example: An entrepreneur uses a DIY platform to register a new LLC with the state, completing the process online without needing to hire a lawyer.

When Not to Use DIY Tools

DIY tools are not suitable for complex legal matters that require specialized expertise. In such cases, it's essential to consult with a qualified legal professional. Here are some scenarios where DIY tools may not be appropriate:

- **Complex Legal Disputes**: Issues involving significant financial stakes, complex legal arguments, or potential litigation.
- **Specialized Legal Advice**: Situations requiring in-depth knowledge of specific legal areas, such as intellectual property law or tax law.
- **Custom Legal Solutions**: Cases that need highly tailored legal documents or agreements that go beyond standard templates.

Example: A business facing a lawsuit for breach of contract should consult with a lawyer rather than relying on DIY tools to manage their legal defense.

How to Use DIY Tools Effectively

1. Choosing the Right Tool

Select a tool that fits your specific needs and ensures that it complies with relevant laws and regulations. Research different options and read customer reviews to assess their reliability and effectiveness.

Example: A small business owner chooses a DIY legal platform like LegalZoom to draft contracts, based on its reputation and positive reviews from other users.

2. Understanding Legal Requirements

Familiarize yourself with the relevant laws and regulations in your jurisdiction to ensure that your documents are compliant and legally enforceable.

Example: A landlord uses a DIY tool to create a lease agreement, ensuring that it complies with local rental laws and regulations to protect their interests and those of the tenant.

3. Reviewing Documents Thoroughly

Even with DIY tools, it's crucial to review documents carefully to avoid errors or omissions. Seek legal advice if you have any doubts or concerns about the content.

Example: An individual drafting a will using a DIY platform reviews the document carefully and consults with a lawyer to ensure that all legal requirements are met and their wishes are clearly documented.

4. Using Templates Appropriately

Utilize the templates provided by DIY tools, but customize them to fit your specific needs. Ensure that the document addresses all relevant aspects of your legal matter.

Example: A consultant uses a service contract template from a DIY tool but customizes it to include specific clauses related to confidentiality and project deliverables.

5. Maintaining Security and Confidentiality

Ensure that the DIY tool you choose provides robust security features to protect your legal documents and personal information.

Example: A business owner uses an e-signature tool that offers encryption and secure storage to protect the confidentiality of signed contracts and client data.

Practical Examples of Using DIY Tools

Example 1: E-Signing a Contract

Scenario: A graphic designer needs to sign a contract with a new client for a design project.

Traditional Approach: The designer would print, sign, and scan the contract, then send it back to the client, which could be time-consuming and inconvenient.

DIY Solution: The designer uses an e-signature tool like DocuSign to sign the contract electronically. The client also signs the contract electronically, and both parties receive a copy for their records.

Outcome: The contract is signed quickly and securely, saving time and reducing the need for physical paperwork.

Example 2: Drafting a Rental Agreement

Scenario: A landlord needs to create a rental agreement for a new tenant.

Traditional Approach: The landlord would need to hire a lawyer to draft the agreement, which could be costly and time-consuming.

DIY Solution: The landlord uses a DIY legal tool like LawDepot to select a rental agreement template, customize it with property details and terms, and download the completed agreement for signing.

Outcome: The landlord creates a legally binding rental agreement quickly and affordably, ensuring that the terms are clear and compliant with local laws.

Example 3: Registering a Trademark

Scenario: A small business wants to register a trademark for their new product.

Traditional Approach: The business would need to hire a lawyer to handle the trademark application process, which could be expensive and involve multiple consultations.

DIY Solution: The business uses a DIY platform like LegalZoom to complete the trademark application online, providing all necessary information and documentation.

Outcome: The trademark application is submitted quickly and efficiently, reducing legal costs and helping the business protect its brand.

Example 4: Creating a Will

Scenario: An individual needs to create a will to outline the distribution of their assets.

Traditional Approach: The individual would need to consult with a lawyer to draft the will, which could involve multiple meetings and significant legal fees.

DIY Solution: The individual uses a DIY platform like Rocket Lawyer to select a will template, customize it with their specific instructions, and download the completed will for signing.

Outcome: The individual creates a legally binding will quickly and affordably, ensuring that their estate is managed according to their wishes.

Benefits and Limitations of DIY Tools

Benefits

1. **Cost Savings**: DIY tools are typically more affordable than hiring a lawyer for routine legal tasks.
2. **Convenience**: Handle legal matters online at any time, from any location.
3. **Speed**: Complete legal tasks quickly and efficiently.
4. **Control**: Maintain control over your legal documents and processes.

Example: A startup uses DIY tools to draft and sign contracts quickly and affordably, allowing them to focus on growing their business rather than managing legal paperwork.

Limitations

1. **Legal Complexity**: DIY tools are not suitable for complex legal matters that require specialized expertise.
2. **Compliance**: Users must ensure that their documents comply with relevant laws and regulations.
3. **Customization**: DIY tools may have limited options for customizing documents to fit specific needs.
4. **Security**: Users must choose tools that offer robust security features to protect their data.

Example: An individual using a DIY tool to create a complex trust agreement may find that the tool does not fully address their specific legal needs, requiring consultation with a lawyer.

Conclusion

DIY legal tools provide a valuable resource for handling straightforward legal tasks efficiently and affordably. By understanding how and when to use these tools, you can effectively manage your legal needs and avoid potential pitfalls. Always review documents thoroughly, ensure compliance with relevant laws, and seek legal advice for complex matters. In the next chapter, we will explore the role of artificial intelligence in legal practice and how it is transforming the legal industry.

ENHANCING LEGAL RESOURCE ACCESS: STRATEGIES AND BEST PRACTICES

Introduction to Legal Resource Access

Legal resource access is a fundamental aspect of modern legal practice, providing individuals and organizations with the tools and information necessary to navigate the legal system effectively. The advent of legal technology has significantly enhanced the accessibility of legal resources, democratizing access to legal information and services. In this chapter, we will explore the various facets of legal resource access, including the types of resources available, how technology has transformed access to these resources, and practical examples of their use. This guide is designed to be beginner-friendly, using clear language and real-world examples to illustrate key concepts.

Understanding Legal Resource Access

What is Legal Resource Access?

Legal resource access refers to the ability of individuals and entities to obtain the legal information and tools they need to address legal issues, seek legal remedies, and ensure compliance with laws and regulations. This includes access to legal documents, court records, legal codes, legal advice, and other resources that facilitate understanding and engagement with the legal system.

Example: A small business owner accesses an online legal portal to find information on local business licensing requirements, ensuring compliance without needing to consult a lawyer directly.

Types of Legal Resources

1. Legal Information Portals

Legal information portals provide access to a wide range of legal information, including statutes, case law, regulations, and legal guides. These portals often offer searchable databases that allow users to find relevant legal information quickly and easily.

Example: An individual uses a legal information portal like FindLaw to research state laws on tenant rights, helping them understand their legal position in a rental dispute.

Illustration:

- **Tool**: FindLaw

- **Usage**: The user searches for tenant rights information, reviews legal articles, and accesses relevant statutes to better understand their rights and obligations.

2. Legal Knowledge Platforms

Legal knowledge platforms offer comprehensive resources for legal research, including access to legal texts, commentary, and analysis. These platforms are often used by legal professionals and students to conduct in-depth legal research.

Example: A law student uses a legal knowledge platform like LexisNexis to research case law for a term paper, accessing a wealth of legal information and expert commentary.

Illustration:

- **Tool**: LexisNexis
- **Usage**: The student searches for case law, reads legal analyses, and downloads relevant documents to support their research.

3. Online Dispute Resolution (ODR)

ODR platforms allow parties to resolve disputes online, providing a convenient and efficient alternative to traditional court proceedings. These platforms facilitate mediation and arbitration processes, making legal recourse more accessible.

Example: Two businesses use an ODR platform to resolve a contract dispute, saving time and money compared to traditional litigation.

Illustration:

- **Tool**: Modria
- **Usage**: The businesses submit their dispute to the platform, participate in virtual mediation sessions, and reach a resolution without needing to go to court.

4. Legal Chatbots

Legal chatbots use artificial intelligence (AI) to provide legal assistance through a conversational interface. They can answer legal questions, generate documents, and direct users to relevant legal resources, offering quick and affordable legal help.

Example: An individual uses a legal chatbot to get information about filing a small claims case, receiving step-by-step guidance and relevant forms.

Illustration:

- **Tool**: DoNotPay
- **Usage**: The user interacts with the chatbot to ask questions about small claims court, receives automated responses, and downloads necessary forms.

5. Legal Marketplaces

Legal marketplaces connect users with legal service providers, allowing them to find and hire lawyers for specific legal tasks. These platforms provide access to a variety of legal services, from document review to legal representation.

Example: A startup uses a legal marketplace to find a lawyer for trademark registration, comparing prices and reviews to choose the best service provider.

Illustration:

- **Tool**: UpCounsel
- **Usage**: The startup searches for trademark lawyers, reviews profiles and client ratings, and hires a lawyer to handle their trademark application.

Benefits of Legal Technology in Resource Access

Enhanced Accessibility

Legal technology has made it easier for individuals to access legal information and services from anywhere, at any time. This increased accessibility helps people understand their legal rights and take appropriate actions.

Example: An individual living in a remote area uses an online legal portal to access legal information that would otherwise be difficult to obtain, helping them navigate a legal issue without needing to travel to a law library.

Cost-Effectiveness

Legal tech solutions often provide more affordable options for obtaining legal services and information, reducing the financial barriers to accessing legal recourse.

Example: A small business saves money by using a legal marketplace to find affordable legal advice for contract drafting, avoiding the higher costs of traditional legal services.

Convenience and Efficiency

Technology enables quicker access to legal resources, streamlining the process of obtaining legal information and assistance. This efficiency is particularly valuable for resolving time-sensitive legal matters.

Example: An individual facing a legal deadline uses an ODR platform to resolve a dispute quickly, avoiding the delays associated with traditional court proceedings.

Democratization of Legal Knowledge

By providing open access to legal information and resources, legal technology helps level the playing field, making legal knowledge more accessible to people from diverse backgrounds and economic circumstances.

Example: A student from a low-income background uses a free legal information portal to study for their law exams, accessing the same resources as their peers without the need for expensive textbooks or subscriptions.

Practical Examples of Legal Resource Access

Example 1: Accessing Legal Codes and Regulations

Scenario: A nonprofit organization needs to ensure compliance with local regulations for a new community project.

Traditional Approach: The organization would need to consult with a lawyer or access physical legal libraries to find the relevant information, which could be time-consuming and costly.

Tech Solution: The organization uses a legal information portal like FindLaw to access local regulations online, reviewing the requirements for their project.

Outcome: The organization quickly obtains the necessary legal information, ensuring compliance without incurring significant legal costs.

Example 2: Resolving a Consumer Dispute Online

Scenario: An individual has a dispute with a retailer over a faulty product and seeks a resolution without going to court.

Traditional Approach: The individual would need to file a complaint with a consumer protection agency or take legal action, which could be lengthy and complex.

Tech Solution: The individual uses an ODR platform like Modria to submit the dispute and participate in online mediation, reaching a settlement with the retailer.

Outcome: The dispute is resolved quickly and efficiently, without the need for formal legal proceedings.

Example 3: Finding Legal Representation for a Startup

Scenario: A startup needs legal assistance for incorporating the business and drafting contracts.

Traditional Approach: The startup would need to search for a lawyer through traditional means, such as referrals or advertisements, which could be time-consuming and uncertain.

Tech Solution: The startup uses a legal marketplace like UpCounsel to find and hire a lawyer with expertise in startup law, reviewing profiles and client ratings.

Outcome: The startup finds a qualified lawyer quickly and affordably, ensuring that their legal needs are met efficiently.

Example 4: Generating Legal Documents with a Chatbot

Scenario: An individual needs to create a simple will but cannot afford a lawyer.

Traditional Approach: The individual would need to consult with a lawyer to draft the will, which could be expensive and involve multiple consultations.

Tech Solution: The individual uses a legal chatbot like DoNotPay to generate a will, providing information through a conversational interface and receiving a customized document.

Outcome: The individual creates a legally binding will quickly and at no cost, ensuring that their wishes are clearly documented.

Challenges and Considerations

Quality and Reliability

While legal tech solutions provide valuable access to resources, it's important to ensure that the information is accurate and reliable. Users should verify the credibility of the platforms and tools they use.

Example: An individual using a legal information portal should check the sources of the information and ensure that it is up-to-date and from a reputable provider.

Security and Privacy

Legal tech platforms must provide robust security measures to protect sensitive legal information and maintain user confidentiality.

Example: A business using an ODR platform should ensure that the platform uses encryption and other security measures to protect the confidentiality of their dispute resolution process.

Understanding Limitations

DIY legal tools and online resources are best suited for straightforward legal tasks and may not be appropriate for complex legal issues that require professional expertise.

Example: An individual facing a complicated legal dispute should seek advice from a qualified lawyer rather than relying solely on a DIY legal tool.

Conclusion

Legal technology has transformed access to legal resources, making it easier, more affordable, and more convenient for individuals and organizations to navigate the legal system. By understanding the various types of legal resources available and how to use them effectively, you can take advantage of these tools to address your legal needs efficiently. In the next chapter, we will explore the role of artificial intelligence in legal practice and how it is revolutionizing the legal industry.

LEGAL INFORMATION PORTALS: FEATURES, BENEFITS, AND USAGE TIPS

Introduction to Legal Information Portals

Legal information portals have become indispensable tools in the legal field, providing easy access to a vast array of legal resources. These platforms offer a convenient, affordable, and efficient way for legal professionals, students, and the general public to access legal information, conduct research, and stay updated with legal developments. This chapter will explore the key features of legal information portals, their benefits, and how to use them effectively. We will also provide practical examples and a case study to illustrate their application in real-world scenarios.

Understanding Legal Information Portals

What Are Legal Information Portals?

Legal information portals are online platforms that aggregate a wide range of legal resources, including statutes, case law, regulations, legal commentary, and scholarly articles. These portals often provide advanced search functionalities, enabling users to find relevant legal information quickly and efficiently.

Example: A law student uses a legal information portal like LexisNexis to access a database of case law and legal journals for a research paper.

Key Features of Legal Information Portals

1. Comprehensive Legal Databases

Legal information portals offer access to extensive databases that include statutes, case law, regulations, and legal commentary. These databases are often updated regularly to ensure that users have access to the most current legal information.

Example: The Legal Information Institute (LII) at Cornell Law School provides open access to US federal and state legislation, case law, rules, legal commentary, and legal forms.

2. Advanced Search Capabilities

These portals feature robust search tools that allow users to locate specific legal information efficiently. Advanced search options may include keyword searches, Boolean searches, citation searches, and filters by jurisdiction, date, or document type.

Example: A lawyer uses Westlaw's KeyCite feature to check the validity of a legal citation and find related case law.

3. Legal Commentary and Analysis

Many legal information portals offer legal commentary and analysis, helping users understand complex legal issues and stay informed about recent legal trends and developments.

Example: Justia provides free access to legal publications, federal and state legislation, a legal blog, legal forms, and links to legal services.

4. User-Friendly Interfaces

Legal information portals are designed to be user-friendly, with intuitive interfaces that make it easy for users to navigate and find the information they need.

Example: FindLaw offers a simple and accessible interface, allowing users to search for case law, legal news, publications, federal and state legislation, and legal forms.

5. Accessibility and Affordability

These portals provide affordable or free access to legal information, making it accessible to a broader audience, including those who may not have the means to pay for traditional legal resources.

Example: Indian Kanoon is a free legal information portal that provides access to judgments from Indian courts with advanced search options.

Benefits of Legal Information Portals

Enhanced Accessibility

Legal information portals make it possible for individuals and professionals to access legal information from anywhere, at any time, removing geographical and financial barriers.

Example: An individual in a rural area uses an online legal portal to access legal information that would otherwise be difficult to obtain without traveling to a law library.

Cost-Effectiveness

These portals offer a cost-effective alternative to traditional legal resources, reducing the financial burden associated with accessing legal information.

Example: A startup saves money by using a free legal information portal to research trademark registration requirements instead of hiring a lawyer for preliminary research.

Convenience and Efficiency

Legal information portals streamline the process of finding legal information, allowing users to quickly locate relevant documents and resources, saving time and effort.

Example: A paralegal uses an advanced search feature on LexisNexis to quickly find case law relevant to an ongoing case, reducing the time spent on manual research.

Up-to-Date Information

These portals are regularly updated to ensure that users have access to the latest legal developments, statutes, and case law.

Example: The GOV.UK portal provides current and reliable legal information on UK legislation, case law, and advice on various subjects.

Practical Examples of Using Legal Information Portals

Example 1: Conducting Legal Research

Scenario: A law student needs to conduct research on environmental law for a term paper.

Traditional Approach: The student would need to spend hours in a law library, searching through physical books and journals to find relevant information.

Tech Solution: The student uses LexisNexis to access a comprehensive database of legal texts, case law, and scholarly articles on environmental law.

Outcome: The student completes their research more quickly and thoroughly, using advanced search tools to find and analyze relevant legal information.

Example 2: Finding a Specific Case

Scenario: A lawyer needs to find a specific case to support a legal argument in court.

Traditional Approach: The lawyer would manually search through case law books and legal databases, which could be time-consuming.

Tech Solution: The lawyer uses FindLaw to search for the case by name, citation, or keyword, quickly locating the full text of the case and related legal commentary.

Outcome: The lawyer finds the case efficiently, ensuring that they are well-prepared for court.

Example 3: Preparing a Legal Brief

Scenario: A paralegal is tasked with preparing a legal brief for a complex litigation case.

Traditional Approach: The paralegal would need to spend considerable time manually searching for relevant case law and legal publications to support the brief.

Tech Solution: The paralegal uses Westlaw to conduct legal research, using advanced search tools to locate pertinent case law and legal publications.

Outcome: The paralegal prepares a comprehensive legal brief more efficiently, ensuring that all relevant legal information is included.

Case Study: Using Legal Information Portals for Asylum Research

Scenario

Jeeves, a paralegal at a law firm in the UK, is tasked with researching asylum requirements and relevant case law for a client seeking asylum.

Steps Taken

1. **Identify the Legal Information Needed**: Jeeves determines that he needs to research the legal requirements for asylum and find relevant case law on asylum claims.

2. **Choose a Legal Information Portal**: Jeeves selects GOV.UK, which offers access to legislation, case law, and advice on various subjects, including asylum.

3. **Use Search Tools**: Jeeves uses keywords like "asylum," "refugee," "immigration," and "entering and staying" in the search box to find relevant information.

4. **Review Results**: Jeeves reviews the search results, looking for documents that provide detailed information on asylum requirements and relevant case law.

5. **Evaluate Information**: Jeeves evaluates the legal material to ensure its accuracy and relevance, using legal research tools to validate citations and find related legal information.

Outcome

Jeeves efficiently gathers the necessary legal information on asylum requirements and relevant case law, presenting it to his superior to support the client's case. Without the use of GOV.UK, Jeeves' research would have been more time-consuming and less efficient.

Conclusion

Legal information portals are invaluable resources that have revolutionized the way legal information is accessed and used. By providing comprehensive, affordable, and convenient access to legal resources, these portals support legal professionals, students, and the general public in their legal endeavors. Understanding how to use these tools effectively can enhance your legal research, improve efficiency, and ensure that you stay informed about the latest legal developments. In the next chapter, we will explore the role of artificial intelligence in legal practice and how it is transforming the legal industry.

ONLINE DISPUTE RESOLUTION (ODR) UNCOVERED: BENEFITS AND KEY FEATURES

Introduction to Online Dispute Resolution

Online dispute resolution (ODR) platforms are transforming the way disputes are resolved by utilizing digital technology to settle disagreements outside of traditional courtrooms. These platforms offer various approaches such as mediation, negotiation, and arbitration, making it easier and more cost-effective for parties to resolve their conflicts. This chapter will provide a detailed overview of ODR platforms, their benefits, and practical applications, with illustrative examples to help beginners understand their use and significance in the legal field.

Understanding Online Dispute Resolution

What is Online Dispute Resolution?

Online dispute resolution (ODR) refers to the use of digital technology to facilitate the resolution of disputes between parties. ODR encompasses various methods, including mediation, negotiation, and arbitration, all conducted online, which eliminates the need for physical meetings and paper-based documentation.

Example: Two businesses involved in a contract dispute use an ODR platform to negotiate a settlement agreement online, avoiding the costs and time associated with traditional litigation.

Key Features of ODR Platforms

1. Secure Communication Tools

ODR platforms provide secure communication channels such as encrypted messaging and video conferencing to ensure confidentiality and build trust between parties.

Example: A consumer and a retailer use encrypted messaging on an ODR platform to discuss a refund dispute, ensuring their communication remains private.

2. Document Sharing and Evidence Tracking

These platforms offer tools for real-time exchange of relevant information and documents, along with features to track evidence and monitor case progress.

Example: Parties involved in a family law dispute upload and share documents such as financial statements and custody agreements on the platform, allowing both sides to review and present their case effectively.

3. Case Management

ODR platforms include case management tools that facilitate efficient handling of disputes, including payment processing and invoicing features for transparency and financial handling.

Example: A mediator uses the case management tools on an ODR platform to schedule sessions, track case developments, and manage payments from the disputing parties.

4. Customization and Flexibility

These platforms often allow for customization to cater to the unique needs of different types of disputes, providing flexible solutions that can include negotiation, mediation, arbitration, or a hybrid approach.

Example: A startup uses a customizable ODR platform to handle intellectual property disputes, selecting a combination of mediation and arbitration to resolve conflicts efficiently.

Types of ODR Platforms

Negotiation-Based Platforms

Negotiation-based ODR platforms facilitate direct communication between parties to help them negotiate and reach an agreement independently.

Example: A tenant and landlord use a negotiation-based platform to discuss and resolve a rent dispute without the need for a mediator or arbitrator.

Mediation-Based Platforms

Mediation-based platforms involve a neutral third party (mediator) who facilitates communication and helps parties reach a mutually acceptable solution.

Example: Two companies involved in a partnership dispute use a mediation-based platform where a mediator assists them in finding a compromise that works for both sides.

Arbitration-Based Platforms

Arbitration-based platforms involve an arbitrator who acts as a judge and makes a binding decision based on the evidence presented by the parties.

Example: An employee and employer use an arbitration-based platform to resolve a wrongful termination claim, with the arbitrator issuing a final decision.

Hybrid Platforms

Hybrid platforms combine elements of negotiation, mediation, and arbitration to provide a tailored approach that meets the specific needs of the parties involved.

Example: A construction company and a subcontractor use a hybrid ODR platform that starts with negotiation, moves to mediation if needed, and ends with arbitration if no agreement is reached.

Benefits of Online Dispute Resolution

Efficiency and Cost-Effectiveness

ODR platforms reduce the need for physical meetings, travel, and paper-based documentation, making the dispute resolution process more efficient and cost-effective.

Example: A freelancer and a client use an ODR platform to settle a payment dispute quickly and affordably, avoiding the expenses associated with traditional legal proceedings.

Convenience and Accessibility

ODR platforms allow parties to resolve disputes remotely, providing convenience and accessibility regardless of their location or mobility issues.

Example: An elderly couple uses an ODR platform to resolve a property boundary dispute with their neighbor, avoiding the need to attend in-person meetings.

Better Outcomes and Satisfaction

ODR can lead to better outcomes and higher satisfaction levels for parties by providing a more flexible and less adversarial process compared to traditional court proceedings.

Example: A divorced couple uses an ODR platform for child custody mediation, finding a solution that prioritizes the best interests of their children and is agreeable to both parties.

Impact on the Legal Industry

ODR showcases the impact of technology on the legal industry by improving efficiency, transparency, and accuracy in dispute resolution processes.

Example: Courts and legal professionals integrate ODR platforms into their services to handle small claims and civil disputes more efficiently, reducing caseloads and speeding up the resolution process.

Practical Examples of ODR Platforms

Example 1: eBay's Resolution Center

Scenario: A buyer and seller on eBay have a dispute over a damaged item received by the buyer.

Traditional Approach: The buyer would need to file a complaint with eBay, which could involve lengthy email exchanges and delays.

ODR Solution: The buyer and seller use eBay's Resolution Center, an ODR platform that facilitates communication and resolution of the dispute. The platform guides them through the process of providing evidence and negotiating a settlement.

Outcome: The dispute is resolved quickly and efficiently, with the buyer receiving a refund and the seller maintaining their reputation.

Example 2: Modria

Scenario: Two businesses have a contract dispute and want to avoid the costs and time associated with traditional litigation.

Traditional Approach: The businesses would need to hire lawyers and go through the court system, which could be costly and time-consuming.

ODR Solution: The businesses use Modria, an ODR platform that provides professional mediators to help them reach a resolution. They communicate through secure messaging and video conferencing, sharing documents and evidence on the platform.

Outcome: The dispute is resolved efficiently, saving both businesses time and money.

Example 3: Civil Resolution Tribunal (CRT) in British Columbia

Scenario: An individual has a small claim against a contractor for incomplete work.

Traditional Approach: The individual would need to file a claim in small claims court, attend hearings, and potentially hire a lawyer.

ODR Solution: The individual uses the Civil Resolution Tribunal (CRT), an online tribunal for small claims and strata property disputes. The platform provides tools for negotiation, mediation, and a formal tribunal decision if needed.

Outcome: The individual resolves the dispute online, saving time and avoiding the need for court appearances.

Example 4: Resolver

Scenario: A customer has a complaint about poor service from an airline and seeks compensation.

Traditional Approach: The customer would need to file a complaint with the airline, which could involve lengthy phone calls and email exchanges.

ODR Solution: The customer uses Resolver, an ODR platform that helps them file a complaint and communicate with the airline. The platform guides the customer through the process and provides templates for documenting the complaint.

Outcome: The complaint is resolved quickly, with the airline providing compensation and the customer avoiding the hassle of traditional complaint processes.

Challenges and Considerations

Lack of Personal Interaction

ODR may lack the personal interaction that some parties prefer, which can be a challenge in disputes that require a more human touch.

Example: In family law disputes involving sensitive issues, parties may prefer in-person mediation to ensure a more personal and empathetic approach.

Concerns About Impartiality

Parties may have concerns about the impartiality and fairness of the mediator or arbitrator selected by the platform.

Example: Businesses using an arbitration-based ODR platform may worry about the neutrality of the arbitrator if there is no transparency in the selection process.

Limited Scope

ODR may not be suitable for all types of legal disputes, particularly those involving complex legal issues or significant financial stakes.

Example: A complex intellectual property dispute involving multiple jurisdictions may require specialized legal expertise and traditional court proceedings.

Standardization and Regulation

There is a need for standardized processes and regulations to ensure the reliability and effectiveness of ODR platforms.

Example: Governments and legal bodies must establish clear guidelines and standards for ODR platforms to ensure they meet legal and ethical requirements.

Conclusion

Online dispute resolution platforms are revolutionizing the way disputes are resolved, offering efficient, cost-effective, and accessible solutions. By understanding the key features, benefits, and practical applications of these platforms, legal professionals and individuals can leverage ODR to resolve disputes more effectively. As technology continues to advance, the role of ODR in the legal industry is expected to grow, providing greater access to justice for a wider range of disputes. In the next chapter, we will explore the role of artificial intelligence in legal practice and how it is transforming the legal industry.

LEGAL CHATBOTS: FEATURES, BENEFITS, AND REAL-WORLD APPLICATIONS

Introduction to Legal Chatbots

Legal chatbots are transforming the legal industry by providing automated, efficient, and accessible legal services. These AI-powered tools simulate human conversation to offer legal information, assist with document generation, and perform various other legal tasks. This chapter will explore the key features, benefits, and applications of legal chatbots, providing practical examples to illustrate their use. Designed for beginners, this guide aims to simplify the concept of legal chatbots, making it easy to understand and apply.

Understanding Legal Chatbots

What Are Legal Chatbots?

Legal chatbots are AI-driven programs designed to simulate conversation with users through text or voice interactions. They can perform various legal tasks, such as answering legal questions, generating documents, and assisting with legal research, making legal services more accessible and efficient.

Example: A person looking for information on how to file for divorce can use a legal chatbot to receive guidance, access relevant forms, and understand the legal process.

How Do Legal Chatbots Work?

Legal chatbots use natural language processing (NLP) to understand and interpret user queries, providing relevant responses based on pre-programmed rules and AI algorithms. They can be integrated into websites, mobile apps, and messaging platforms, offering 24/7 accessibility.

Example: A legal chatbot on a law firm's website helps visitors by answering common legal questions and directing them to appropriate resources or attorneys.

Key Features of Legal Chatbots

1. Natural Language Processing (NLP)

NLP enables chatbots to understand and respond to user inputs in a human-like manner. This technology allows chatbots to interpret the intent behind queries and provide accurate responses.

Example: A chatbot uses NLP to understand a user's question about tenant rights and provides relevant information based on local laws.

2. Automated Document Generation

Legal chatbots can generate legal documents, such as contracts, wills, and non-disclosure agreements, based on user inputs. This feature saves time and reduces errors associated with manual document creation.

Example: A small business owner uses a legal chatbot to generate a customized employment contract by answering a series of questions about the job role and terms.

3. Secure Data Handling

Chatbots ensure that all user interactions and data are handled securely, complying with data protection regulations to maintain confidentiality and trust.

Example: A chatbot integrated into a legal firm's system uses encryption to protect sensitive client information during interactions.

4. Integration with Legal Databases

Legal chatbots can access and retrieve information from legal databases, providing users with up-to-date legal information and case law.

Example: A chatbot helps a lawyer by quickly retrieving relevant case law from a legal database based on specific keywords and citations.

Benefits of Legal Chatbots

Efficiency and Time Savings

Legal chatbots automate routine tasks, allowing legal professionals to focus on more complex and billable work. This increases overall efficiency and reduces the time spent on repetitive tasks.

Example: A law firm uses a chatbot to handle initial client inquiries and appointment bookings, freeing up staff to work on active cases.

Accessibility and Convenience

Chatbots provide legal assistance anytime and anywhere, making legal services more accessible to individuals who may not have easy access to traditional legal resources.

Example: An individual in a remote area uses a chatbot to get legal advice on a property dispute, without needing to travel to a law office.

Cost-Effectiveness

By automating various legal processes, chatbots reduce the cost of legal services, making them more affordable for clients.

Example: A startup saves money by using a chatbot to draft standard legal documents instead of hiring a lawyer for each document.

Consistency and Accuracy

Chatbots provide consistent and accurate information, minimizing the risk of human error and ensuring that users receive reliable legal guidance.

Example: A chatbot provides consistent information on the steps to file a small claims court case, ensuring that all users follow the correct procedures.

Practical Examples of Legal Chatbots

Example 1: DoNotPay

Scenario: An individual wants to contest a parking ticket but is unsure of the process.

Traditional Approach: The individual would need to research the procedure, draft an appeal letter, and submit it manually.

Chatbot Solution: DoNotPay, a legal chatbot, guides the user through the process of contesting a parking ticket, generating an appeal letter based on the user's inputs.

Outcome: The individual successfully contests the parking ticket with minimal effort, thanks to the guidance and document generation provided by the chatbot.

Example 2: LawDroid

Scenario: A law firm needs to streamline its client intake process.

Traditional Approach: The firm would manually handle client inquiries, collect information, and schedule appointments, which could be time-consuming.

Chatbot Solution: The firm implements LawDroid, a legal chatbot that automates client intake by answering initial inquiries, collecting client information, and booking appointments.

Outcome: The firm improves efficiency, reduces administrative workload, and provides a better client experience.

Example 3: LegalZoom Chatbot

Scenario: An entrepreneur needs to register a new business but is unsure of the legal requirements.

Traditional Approach: The entrepreneur would need to consult with a lawyer or conduct extensive research to understand the registration process.

Chatbot Solution: The LegalZoom chatbot provides step-by-step guidance on business registration, including required documents and filing procedures.

Outcome: The entrepreneur registers the business quickly and easily, with clear guidance from the chatbot.

Example 4: IBM Watson Legal

Scenario: A lawyer needs to conduct legal research on a specific topic.

Traditional Approach: The lawyer would spend hours searching through legal databases and documents to find relevant information.

Chatbot Solution: IBM Watson Legal, an AI-powered chatbot, assists the lawyer by quickly retrieving relevant case law and legal documents based on the lawyer's queries.

Outcome: The lawyer completes the research more efficiently, saving time and accessing comprehensive legal information.

Challenges and Considerations

Ensuring Accuracy and Reliability

While chatbots can provide accurate information, it is essential to regularly update their databases and algorithms to ensure they remain reliable and compliant with current laws.

Example: A legal firm using a chatbot must regularly update the chatbot's database with new legal precedents and regulations to ensure accurate responses.

Addressing Privacy Concerns

Legal chatbots must handle sensitive information securely, complying with data protection laws and ensuring user confidentiality.

Example: A chatbot handling client information must use encryption and secure data storage to protect user privacy.

Managing Complex Queries

While chatbots can handle many routine tasks, they may struggle with complex legal queries that require human expertise.

Example: A chatbot can provide basic information on filing for divorce but may refer users to a lawyer for complex cases involving custody disputes or significant assets.

Integrating with Existing Systems

Integrating chatbots with existing legal systems and workflows can be challenging but is necessary for seamless operation and maximum efficiency.

Example: A law firm must ensure that its chatbot integrates with its case management system to streamline client interactions and document handling.

Conclusion

Legal chatbots are revolutionizing the legal industry by automating routine tasks, providing accessible legal information, and improving overall efficiency. By understanding the key features, benefits, and practical applications of legal chatbots, legal professionals and individuals can leverage these tools to enhance their legal services. As technology continues to advance, the role of legal chatbots is expected to grow, providing even more sophisticated and valuable legal assistance. In the next chapter, we will explore the role of artificial intelligence in legal practice and how it is transforming the legal industry.

LEGAL MARKETPLACES EXPLAINED: TYPES, BENEFITS, AND USES

Introduction to Legal Marketplaces

Legal marketplaces are online platforms that connect legal professionals with consumers and potential clients seeking legal services. These marketplaces offer a wide range of legal services, including document drafting, contract review, and legal advice. They have revolutionized the traditional legal industry by making legal services more accessible, affordable, and convenient. This chapter will provide an in-depth overview of legal marketplaces, discussing their types, benefits, and practical applications with illustrative examples to help beginners understand and utilize these platforms effectively.

Understanding Legal Marketplaces

What Are Legal Marketplaces?

Legal marketplaces are digital platforms that facilitate connections between legal service providers and clients. They offer various services, from simple DIY legal solutions to complex legal advice and representation. These platforms can be broadly grouped into commoditized legal solution marketplaces and electronic marketplaces that connect consumers directly to lawyers.

Example: A small business owner uses a legal marketplace to find a lawyer who can help with incorporating their business and drafting necessary contracts.

Importance of Legal Marketplaces in the Legal Industry

Legal marketplaces have disrupted the traditional legal industry by providing consumers with affordable and convenient access to legal services. They also create new opportunities for legal professionals to expand their client base and grow their businesses.

Example: A freelance lawyer uses a legal marketplace to reach potential clients who need legal services but may not have considered hiring a traditional law firm.

Types of Legal Marketplaces

A. Commoditized Legal Solution Marketplaces

These marketplaces offer standardized legal services and document creation tools, primarily through DIY solutions. Users can generate legal documents and access simple legal advice without hiring a lawyer.

Example: LegalZoom and Rocket Lawyer provide online legal document services that allow users to create wills, contracts, and other legal forms.

B. Electronic Marketplaces and Multisided Platforms

These platforms connect consumers directly with legal professionals for more personalized legal services. They include both B2B (business-to-business) and B2C (business-to-consumer) services.

1. B2B Legal Marketplaces

B2B legal marketplaces connect businesses with legal professionals and other businesses needing legal services. They offer a range of services, including recruiting, legal databases, insourcing, and legal process outsourcing (LPO).

Example: UpCounsel connects businesses with freelance lawyers for various legal tasks, such as contract review and intellectual property protection.

2. B2C Legal Marketplaces

B2C legal marketplaces connect individual clients with legal professionals. They offer services like online listings, reputation comparisons, legal advice, and fixed-fee legal packages.

Example: Avvo provides a platform where individuals can find and compare lawyers, read reviews, and book appointments for legal consultations.

Benefits of Legal Marketplaces

For Clients

Cost-Effectiveness

Legal marketplaces offer more affordable legal services compared to traditional law firms by streamlining processes and reducing overhead costs.

Example: An individual uses a legal marketplace to draft a simple will at a fraction of the cost of hiring a lawyer.

Increased Convenience

Clients can access legal services online from their homes or offices, making it easier to get legal help without the need for physical visits to law firms.

Example: A busy professional uses an online platform to book a consultation with a lawyer during their lunch break.

Access to a Broader Pool of Legal Professionals

Legal marketplaces provide access to a wide range of legal professionals with different specialties and experience levels, making it easier to find the right lawyer for specific needs.

Example: A startup founder uses a legal marketplace to find a lawyer specializing in intellectual property law to help with patent filings.

For Legal Professionals

Increased Exposure and Visibility

Legal marketplaces connect legal professionals with a wider audience of potential clients, helping them expand their client base and grow their practice.

Example: A newly licensed lawyer uses a legal marketplace to reach clients who need affordable legal services.

Streamlined Billing and Payment Processes

These platforms often include tools for managing billing and payments, making it easier for legal professionals to get paid quickly and efficiently.

Example: A freelance lawyer uses a legal marketplace's integrated payment system to invoice clients and receive payments without delay.

Practical Examples of Legal Marketplaces

Example 1: LegalZoom for Document Creation

Scenario: A couple needs to create a will and living trust.

Traditional Approach: The couple would hire a lawyer to draft these documents, which could be costly and time-consuming.

Marketplace Solution: The couple uses LegalZoom to create their will and living trust online, using templates and guided prompts to customize their documents.

Outcome: The couple completes their legal documents quickly and affordably, ensuring their wishes are legally documented.

Example 2: UpCounsel for Business Legal Services

Scenario: A tech startup needs legal advice on intellectual property protection and contract review.

Traditional Approach: The startup would need to hire a full-time in-house lawyer or engage a law firm, both of which could be expensive.

Marketplace Solution: The startup uses UpCounsel to find freelance lawyers specializing in intellectual property and contract law, engaging them on an as-needed basis.

Outcome: The startup receives expert legal advice and services at a lower cost, helping them protect their intellectual property and draft effective contracts.

Example 3: Avvo for Finding Legal Representation

Scenario: An individual is facing a legal issue and needs to find a reputable lawyer.

Traditional Approach: The individual would rely on referrals or conduct extensive searches to find a suitable lawyer, which could be time-consuming and uncertain.

Marketplace Solution: The individual uses Avvo to search for lawyers, read client reviews, and compare ratings to find the best fit for their legal needs.

Outcome: The individual quickly finds a highly-rated lawyer, books a consultation, and receives the legal representation they need.

Challenges and Limitations of Legal Marketplaces

Ethical and Regulatory Compliance

Legal marketplaces must comply with ethical and regulatory requirements, including client confidentiality and avoiding conflicts of interest. They must ensure that legal professionals using their platform are licensed and in good standing with their state bar association.

Example: A legal marketplace verifies the credentials of lawyers before allowing them to offer services on the platform, ensuring compliance with regulatory standards.

Quality Control and Accountability

Ensuring the quality of legal services provided through these platforms is crucial. Marketplaces often use client reviews, background checks, and skills assessments to maintain high standards.

Example: A legal marketplace uses a rating system and client feedback to monitor the performance of lawyers, ensuring that only high-quality services are offered.

Impact on Traditional Legal Industry

Legal marketplaces may disrupt traditional law firms by offering lower prices and greater convenience, posing a competitive threat to traditional legal practices.

Example: Traditional law firms may need to adopt new technologies and business models to compete with the affordable and accessible services offered by legal marketplaces.

Conclusion

Legal marketplaces are transforming the legal industry by providing accessible, affordable, and convenient legal services. By understanding the different types of legal marketplaces and their benefits, both clients and legal professionals can effectively utilize these platforms to meet their legal needs. As technology continues to advance, legal marketplaces are expected to play an increasingly important role in the legal sector, offering innovative solutions and expanding access to justice. In the next chapter, we will explore the role of artificial intelligence in legal practice and how it is revolutionizing the legal industry.

DATA SCIENCE AND COMPUTATIONAL LAW: APPLICATIONS AND INNOVATIONS

Introduction to Data Science and Computational Law

Data science and computational law are two emerging fields that are transforming the legal industry by leveraging technology to analyze, predict, and optimize legal processes. Data science involves using scientific methods, algorithms, and systems to extract knowledge and insights from structured and unstructured data. Computational law, on the other hand, combines computer science, artificial intelligence, and legal theory to create systems that can automate legal analysis, decision-making, and compliance. This chapter will explore these concepts, their applications, and provide practical examples to illustrate their impact on the legal industry.

Understanding Data Science in Law

What is Data Science?

Data science is the study of extracting information and insights from data through scientific methods, algorithms, and systems. It involves various disciplines such as mathematics, statistics, computer science, and domain knowledge—in this case, legal knowledge. Data science processes, analyzes, and visualizes data to uncover patterns, trends, and correlations that aid in informed decision-making.

Example: A law firm uses data science to analyze past case outcomes and identify trends that can help predict the success of future cases.

Applications of Data Science in the Legal Industry

1. Document Review and E-Discovery

Machine learning algorithms can automate the review and analysis of documents, making the e-discovery process more efficient and accurate.

Example: A law firm uses machine learning to scan thousands of emails and documents to identify relevant information for a litigation case, significantly reducing the time and cost of manual review.

2. Legal Research

Data science can automate legal research by analyzing vast amounts of legal texts, case law, and regulations to provide relevant information quickly.

Example: A legal chatbot uses natural language processing (NLP) to search legal databases and provide lawyers with pertinent case law and statutes related to their queries.

3. Contract Analysis

Algorithms can analyze contracts to identify potential issues, inconsistencies, and compliance risks, improving contract management.

Example: A company uses data science tools to review and analyze its contracts for compliance with new regulatory requirements, ensuring that all contracts are updated accordingly.

4. Risk Analysis and Management

Data analytics can help identify and assess risk factors, allowing legal professionals to take proactive measures to manage risks and avoid legal pitfalls.

Example: A legal team uses predictive analytics to assess the risk of litigation for a new business venture, helping the company make informed decisions to mitigate potential legal issues.

5. Predictive Analytics

Predictive models can analyze patterns in case law to forecast case outcomes, aiding lawyers in developing strategies and advising clients.

Example: A lawyer uses predictive analytics to estimate the likelihood of winning a case based on historical data and similar case outcomes.

Understanding Computational Law

What is Computational Law?

Computational law is the field that merges computer science, artificial intelligence, and legal theory to create systems and tools that automate legal analysis, decision-making, and compliance. It uses algorithms, machine learning techniques, and natural language processing to analyze legal data, identify patterns, and generate insights that assist legal professionals in their work.

Example: A law firm develops a computational tool that automates the generation of legal briefs by analyzing relevant case law and statutes, saving time and improving accuracy.

Applications of Computational Law

1. Contract Automation

Computational law enables the creation of smart contracts that automatically execute and enforce contractual obligations based on predefined conditions.

Example: A real estate transaction is facilitated by a smart contract that automatically transfers ownership and funds once all conditions are met, reducing the need for intermediaries and ensuring a secure transaction.

2. Legal Prediction and Decision-Making

Machine learning models can predict legal outcomes and assist in decision-making by analyzing historical data and identifying relevant factors.

Example: A judicial decision support system uses computational law to predict case outcomes based on past judgments, helping judges make more informed decisions.

3. Regulatory Compliance

Computational law tools can monitor and analyze regulatory changes, ensuring that organizations remain compliant with evolving legal requirements.

Example: A financial institution uses a compliance tool that automatically updates its policies and procedures based on new regulatory requirements, reducing the risk of non-compliance.

4. Legal Research and Analysis

Advanced algorithms can perform legal research and analysis, providing insights and recommendations based on large datasets of legal information.

Example: A legal researcher uses a computational tool to analyze trends in case law and identify emerging legal issues, aiding in the development of legal strategies.

Practical Examples

Example 1: Analysis of Prior Cases and Outcome Prediction

Scenario: A law firm wants to predict the outcomes of personal injury cases to provide better advice to clients.

Traditional Approach: The firm would rely on the experience and judgment of its lawyers to estimate the likelihood of success, which can be subjective.

Data Science Solution: The firm uses data science to analyze past personal injury cases, identifying patterns and trends that can predict outcomes. This includes analyzing variables such as the type of injury, jurisdiction, and legal representation.

Outcome: The firm provides clients with data-driven predictions, improving accuracy and helping clients make informed decisions about their cases.

Example 2: Cost Estimation for Legal Cases

Scenario: A client needs to estimate the cost of pursuing a legal case.

Traditional Approach: Estimating costs would involve manually reviewing similar cases and consulting with legal professionals, which can be time-consuming and imprecise.

Data Science Solution: The firm uses machine learning models to analyze historical data and estimate the costs of similar cases, considering factors like case complexity, duration, and legal fees.

Outcome: The client receives a detailed and accurate cost estimate, helping them make informed financial decisions regarding their legal case.

Example 3: Judge Analysis for Consistent Rulings

Scenario: A legal team aims to ensure consistency in legal rulings by analyzing past judgments.

Traditional Approach: Analyzing past judgments manually would be labor-intensive and prone to errors.

Data Science Solution: The team uses data science to analyze patterns in past judgments, identifying factors that influence judicial decisions and ensuring consistency in similar cases.

Outcome: The legal team can make data-driven recommendations to ensure consistent rulings, promoting fairness and transparency in the legal system.

Challenges and Considerations

Data Quality and Preparation

Ensuring the accuracy and reliability of data is crucial for effective data science and computational law applications. This involves data cleaning, validation, and integration from multiple sources.

Example: A law firm invests in data cleaning tools to ensure that their case data is accurate and complete before using it for predictive analytics.

Ethical and Legal Implications

Using data science and computational law raises ethical and legal concerns, such as data privacy, bias in algorithms, and the accountability of automated decisions.

Example: A legal tech company develops guidelines to ensure that its algorithms are free from bias and comply with data protection regulations.

Integration with Existing Legal Systems

Integrating data science and computational tools with existing legal systems and workflows can be challenging but is necessary for seamless operation.

Example: A law firm collaborates with IT professionals to integrate a new predictive analytics tool with their existing case management system.

Conclusion

Data science and computational law are revolutionizing the legal industry by providing tools and techniques that enhance decision-making, improve efficiency, and offer new insights. By understanding and leveraging these technologies, legal professionals can offer more innovative and effective services to their clients. As technology continues to evolve, the role of data science and computational law is expected to expand, further transforming the legal landscape.

ARTIFICIAL INTELLIGENCE (AI) IN LAW: KEY ASPECTS, APPLICATIONS, AND BENEFITS

Introduction to Artificial Intelligence in Law

Artificial intelligence (AI) is revolutionizing various industries, including the legal field. AI encompasses technologies that enable machines to mimic human intelligence, such as learning, problem-solving, and decision-making. In law, AI has the potential to transform how legal services are delivered, making them more efficient, accurate, and accessible. This chapter will explore the key aspects of AI in law, its applications, benefits, and provide practical examples to illustrate its impact on the legal profession.

Understanding Artificial Intelligence

What is Artificial Intelligence?

Artificial Intelligence (AI) refers to the simulation of human intelligence processes by computer systems. These processes include learning (the acquisition of information and rules for using the information), reasoning (using rules to reach approximate or definite conclusions), and self-correction. AI can be categorized into two main types: narrow AI (or weak AI) and general AI (or strong AI).

Example: Narrow AI includes systems designed for specific tasks like legal research, while general AI would have the ability to perform any intellectual task that a human can do, which is currently a theoretical concept.

Key Technologies in AI

- **Machine Learning (ML)**: A subset of AI that involves training algorithms to learn from data and make predictions or decisions.
- **Natural Language Processing (NLP)**: Enables machines to understand and respond to human language.
- **Deep Learning**: A subset of machine learning that uses neural networks to model complex patterns in data.
- **Expert Systems**: AI programs that mimic the decision-making abilities of a human expert.

Applications of AI in Law

1. Legal Research and Document Review

AI-powered tools can automate the process of legal research and document review, significantly reducing the time and effort required to find relevant information and analyze documents.

Example: ROSS Intelligence uses AI to conduct legal research by analyzing vast amounts of legal texts and providing precise answers to legal questions.

2. Predictive Analytics

Predictive analytics involves using data, statistical algorithms, and machine learning techniques to identify the likelihood of future outcomes based on historical data. In law, this can help predict case outcomes and legal trends.

Example: Lex Machina provides legal analytics by examining past case outcomes to predict how a judge might rule in future cases, helping lawyers develop better strategies.

3. Contract Analysis and Management

AI tools can analyze and manage contracts more efficiently by identifying key terms, potential risks, and compliance issues, facilitating faster contract review and negotiation.

Example: Kira Systems uses machine learning to identify and extract important information from contracts, improving the speed and accuracy of contract analysis.

4. Legal Chatbots

AI-driven chatbots provide immediate assistance by answering legal questions, generating documents, and guiding users through legal processes.

Example: DoNotPay, known as the "robot lawyer," helps users contest parking tickets, cancel subscriptions, and handle various legal matters through an easy-to-use chatbot interface.

5. E-Discovery

AI-powered e-discovery tools can sift through large volumes of electronic data to find relevant information for litigation, saving time and reducing costs.

Example: Relativity's e-discovery platform uses AI to automate the identification and categorization of relevant documents in legal cases.

Benefits of AI in Law

Increased Efficiency

AI can process and analyze data much faster than humans, leading to significant time savings in legal research, document review, and case preparation.

Example: A law firm uses AI to review thousands of documents for a litigation case in a fraction of the time it would take human lawyers, allowing them to focus on strategic aspects of the case.

Enhanced Accuracy

AI reduces the risk of human error in legal processes by providing consistent and accurate analysis based on data and algorithms.

Example: An AI tool identifies potential risks in a contract that a human reviewer might overlook, ensuring that all compliance issues are addressed.

Cost Savings

By automating routine tasks, AI can help law firms and legal departments reduce operational costs and offer more affordable legal services to clients.

Example: A small business uses an AI-driven legal platform to draft contracts and manage compliance, avoiding the high costs of hiring a full-time lawyer.

Improved Access to Legal Services

AI-powered legal tools make legal services more accessible to individuals and small businesses that might not afford traditional legal assistance.

Example: Individuals in rural areas use an AI chatbot to get legal advice and document preparation services without traveling to a law office.

Practical Examples of AI in Law

Example 1: Predictive Analytics in Litigation

Scenario: A law firm wants to predict the outcome of a personal injury case to advise their client on whether to settle or proceed to trial.

Traditional Approach: The firm would rely on the experience and intuition of senior lawyers to estimate the likelihood of success, which can be subjective.

AI Solution: The firm uses Lex Machina's predictive analytics tool to analyze past personal injury cases and identify factors that influence case outcomes.

Outcome: The firm provides data-driven advice to the client, increasing the accuracy of their predictions and helping the client make an informed decision.

Example 2: Contract Review and Risk Management

Scenario: A multinational company needs to review thousands of contracts to ensure compliance with new regulatory requirements.

Traditional Approach: The company would assign a team of lawyers to manually review each contract, which could take months and be prone to errors.

AI Solution: The company uses Kira Systems to automate the contract review process, identifying non-compliant clauses and potential risks.

Outcome: The company completes the contract review in weeks instead of months, ensuring compliance and reducing the risk of regulatory penalties.

Example 3: AI Chatbots for Legal Assistance

Scenario: An individual needs to create a will but cannot afford to hire a lawyer.

Traditional Approach: The individual would need to draft the will themselves or find affordable legal assistance, which might not be reliable.

AI Solution: The individual uses DoNotPay's chatbot to generate a legally binding will by answering a series of questions about their estate and wishes.

Outcome: The individual creates a will quickly and affordably, ensuring their estate is managed according to their wishes.

Challenges and Considerations

Ethical and Legal Concerns

The use of AI in law raises ethical and legal concerns, such as data privacy, algorithmic bias, and the accountability of AI decisions. It is essential to address these issues to ensure that AI is used responsibly.

Example: A legal tech company implements strict data privacy measures and regularly audits its algorithms to prevent bias and ensure fairness in AI-driven decisions.

Integration with Existing Systems

Integrating AI tools with existing legal systems and workflows can be challenging but is necessary for seamless operation and maximum efficiency.

Example: A law firm collaborates with IT professionals to integrate an AI-powered legal research tool with their document management system, streamlining the research process.

Training and Adaptation

Legal professionals need training to effectively use AI tools and understand their capabilities and limitations.

Example: A law firm invests in training programs to help lawyers and staff become proficient in using AI-driven legal tools, enhancing their productivity and service quality.

Conclusion

Artificial intelligence is transforming the legal industry by automating routine tasks, enhancing decision-making, and improving access to legal services. By understanding the key applications and benefits of AI in law, legal professionals can leverage these technologies to provide more efficient and effective services to their clients. As AI continues to evolve, its role in the legal sector is expected to grow, offering new opportunities and challenges. In the next chapter, we will explore the ethical implications of AI in law and how to address them.

ROBOT LAWYER, DIGITAL JUSTICE, AND VIRTUAL COURTS: UNDERSTANDING THE TECHNOLOGIES

Introduction to AI and Digital Transformation in Law

Artificial Intelligence (AI) and digital technologies are reshaping the legal landscape, offering innovative solutions for various legal processes. This chapter explores three interconnected topics: robot lawyers, digital justice, and virtual courts. These technologies enhance efficiency, accessibility, and affordability in legal services, making justice more accessible to all. This guide aims to provide a comprehensive understanding of these technologies, illustrated with practical examples to facilitate learning and application for beginners.

Robot Lawyers

What is a Robot Lawyer?

A robot lawyer, also known as an AI lawyer or legal chatbot, is a computer program that uses artificial intelligence to assist with legal tasks such as drafting legal documents, conducting legal research, and providing legal advice. These programs mimic the decision-making process and knowledge of human lawyers, offering cost-effective and efficient legal services.

Example: DoNotPay, an AI legal chatbot, helps users contest parking tickets, make claims for flight delays, and even file lawsuits in small claims court.

Benefits of Robot Lawyers

1. **Cost-Effectiveness**: Robot lawyers offer legal services at a lower cost compared to human lawyers.
2. **Efficiency**: They can complete legal tasks quickly and consistently, minimizing errors.
3. **Accessibility**: Provide legal services to those facing financial or geographical obstacles.
4. **24/7 Availability**: Robot lawyers can work around the clock, providing legal assistance at any time.

Example: Julie, a legal chatbot designed to aid individuals in filing small business claims in Scottish courts, guides users through the process, including adding digital signatures.

Limitations of Robot Lawyers

1. **Lack of Human Judgment**: They may not possess the level of human judgment required in some legal contexts, such as discretion, empathy, and nuanced reasoning.
2. **Technical Issues**: Robot lawyers can encounter technical problems affecting their performance and reliability.
3. **Limited Personal Interaction**: They do not provide the same level of personal interaction as human lawyers.

Example: A contract review platform like LawGeex helps businesses quickly review contracts, but it may struggle with complex legal issues requiring extensive expertise and judgment.

Digital Justice

What is Digital Justice?

Digital justice leverages technology to enhance the accessibility, speed, and efficiency of the justice system. It involves implementing digital platforms to make legal services more accessible, using online dispute resolution to expedite legal disputes, and utilizing technology to improve the efficiency and precision of legal processes.

Example: Online dispute resolution platforms like Modria enable parties to resolve disputes online, providing a convenient and cost-effective alternative to traditional litigation.

Benefits of Digital Justice

1. **Enhanced Access to Justice**: Digital justice technologies provide access to legal information and services to individuals who face barriers such as limited resources or geographical distances.
2. **Transparency and Accountability**: Improve transparency and accountability in the justice system by streamlining legal processes and enhancing access to legal information.
3. **Cost Reduction**: Reduce the costs associated with traditional legal processes, making legal services more affordable and flexible.

Example: Electronic case management systems improve the efficiency of legal processes by digitizing court records and enabling remote access.

Limitations of Digital Justice

1. **Access to Technology**: Limited access to technology can create inequalities and barriers to justice.
2. **Security Concerns**: Security breaches and technical glitches can compromise the reliability and confidentiality of legal information.
3. **Complexity of Legal Issues**: Digital justice technologies may struggle with the complexity of some legal issues, and their reliance on automation can limit personal interaction and the quality of legal advice.

Example: Legal aid platforms provide easier access to legal information and assistance, but may not fully address the complexity of certain legal issues.

Virtual Courts

What are Virtual Courts?

Virtual courts refer to court proceedings conducted remotely using video conferencing and other digital technologies. This allows individuals to participate in legal proceedings from anywhere with an internet connection, making the justice system more accessible and efficient.

Example: Virtual court hearings during the COVID-19 pandemic allowed legal proceedings to continue while minimizing the risk of spreading the virus.

How Virtual Courts Work

1. **Scheduling**: Scheduling court proceedings and sending notifications to participants.
2. **Connection and Setup**: Setting up the necessary connections and ensuring all participants have access to the virtual court platform.
3. **Admittance and Identification**: Verifying the identity of participants and admitting them to the virtual courtroom.
4. **Virtual Proceedings**: Conducting the court proceedings through video conferencing.
5. **Virtual Verdict**: Delivering the ruling by the judge in the virtual courtroom.

Benefits of Virtual Courts

1. **Accessibility**: Enhance accessibility by allowing individuals to participate in legal proceedings remotely.
2. **Cost Savings**: Save costs related to travel, facility rentals, and other expenses associated with traditional court hearings.
3. **Efficiency**: Expedite court proceedings, reducing case backlogs and increasing scheduling flexibility.

Example: Virtual court systems in countries like the UK and India have enabled remote participation in legal proceedings, reducing delays and improving access to justice.

Challenges of Virtual Courts

1. **Technical Issues**: Connectivity problems and compatibility issues between different platforms can disrupt proceedings.
2. **Access to Technology**: Not everyone has access to the necessary digital technologies, creating inequalities.
3. **Perception of Authority**: The lack of physical presence may affect the perception of the court's authority and legitimacy.

Example: Virtual court proceedings in family law cases may limit personal interaction between parties and legal professionals, affecting the quality of legal representation and decision-making.

Practical Examples

Example 1: Robot Lawyer for Small Business Claims

Scenario: A small business owner needs to file a claim in Scottish courts but cannot afford a lawyer.

Traditional Approach: Hiring a lawyer to assist with filing the claim, which could be expensive.

AI Solution: Julie, the legal chatbot, guides the owner through the process of drafting and filing the claim, including adding a digital signature.

Outcome: The owner successfully files the claim at a lower cost and with greater convenience.

Example 2: Online Dispute Resolution for Consumer Disputes

Scenario: A consumer has a dispute with a retailer over a faulty product.

Traditional Approach: Filing a complaint with a consumer protection agency or taking legal action, which could be lengthy and complex.

Digital Justice Solution: Using an online dispute resolution platform like Modria to submit the dispute and participate in virtual mediation.

Outcome: The dispute is resolved quickly and efficiently, saving time and avoiding the need for formal legal proceedings.

Example 3: Virtual Court for Criminal Hearings

Scenario: A defendant in a criminal case needs to attend a hearing during the COVID-19 pandemic.

Traditional Approach: Attending the hearing in person, which could pose health risks.

Virtual Court Solution: The court conducts the hearing remotely using video conferencing technology, allowing the defendant to participate from home.

Outcome: The hearing proceeds safely and efficiently, minimizing the risk of virus transmission and ensuring that justice is served.

Conclusion

The integration of AI and digital technologies in the legal field through robot lawyers, digital justice, and virtual courts is revolutionizing how legal services are delivered. These innovations enhance efficiency, accessibility, and affordability, making justice more accessible to all. However, it is essential to address the challenges and limitations associated with these technologies to ensure they promote fairness, transparency, and accountability in the justice system. As technology continues to evolve, its role in the legal sector is expected to grow, offering new opportunities and challenges for legal professionals and clients alike.

VR AND AR IN LAW: TRANSFORMING LEGAL PRACTICE

Introduction to Virtual and Augmented Reality

Virtual Reality (VR) and Augmented Reality (AR) are innovative technologies that are making significant inroads into various industries, including the legal sector. VR creates a completely simulated environment, while AR overlays digital content onto the real world. These technologies, commonly associated with gaming and entertainment, are now being explored for practical applications in law to enhance training, courtroom experiences, and evidence presentation. This chapter provides a comprehensive overview of VR and AR in the legal field, illustrated with practical examples to help beginners understand their potential and applications.

Understanding Virtual and Augmented Reality

What is Virtual Reality (VR)?

Virtual Reality (VR) is a technology that creates a simulated environment that can be experienced through devices such as headsets or gloves. It immerses users in a completely virtual world, shutting out the physical environment and allowing them to interact with digital objects and scenarios.

Example: Using an Oculus Rift headset, a lawyer can enter a virtual courtroom to practice trial arguments and witness cross-examinations.

What is Augmented Reality (AR)?

Augmented Reality (AR) enhances the real world by overlaying digital content such as images, sounds, and data onto the physical environment. AR can be experienced through devices like smartphones, tablets, and AR glasses.

Example: A lawyer uses AR glasses to visualize crime scene data superimposed onto a real-world location, aiding in better understanding and analysis of the scene.

Applications of VR and AR in Law

1. Simulating Courtroom Environments

VR can simulate courtroom settings, allowing lawyers, judges, and law students to practice and prepare for legal proceedings in a realistic environment. This can help improve their courtroom skills and reduce anxiety.

Example: Law students use VR to simulate a mock trial, where they practice delivering opening statements, examining witnesses, and making closing arguments in a virtual courtroom.

2. Enhanced Evidence Presentation

AR can be used to enhance the presentation of evidence in court by overlaying digital information onto physical objects or scenes. This can help jurors and judges better understand complex evidence.

Example: During a trial, a lawyer uses AR to display a 3D reconstruction of a crime scene on a tablet, allowing the jury to visualize the scene and better understand the evidence.

3. Virtual Reality Crime Scene Recreation

VR can recreate crime scenes, providing an immersive experience for investigators, lawyers, and jurors. This can help in better analyzing and understanding the details of the scene.

Example: Investigators use VR to virtually walk through a recreated crime scene, examining evidence from different perspectives and identifying key details that may have been missed in a traditional investigation.

4. Training and Education

Both VR and AR can be used to create immersive training environments for legal professionals, allowing them to practice and refine their skills in a safe and controlled setting.

Example: Police academies use VR simulators to train officers in handling various scenarios, such as traffic stops, domestic disputes, and active shooter situations, improving their decision-making and response skills.

5. Dispute Resolution

VR can create neutral virtual environments for parties to meet and discuss their disputes, potentially reducing the costs and time associated with traditional in-person mediation or arbitration.

Example: Two companies involved in a commercial dispute use a VR platform to conduct mediation sessions, allowing them to negotiate and resolve their issues without the need for physical meetings.

Benefits of VR and AR in Law

Improved Understanding and Decision-Making

VR and AR provide immersive and interactive experiences that can enhance understanding and decision-making in complex legal cases.

Example: A jury uses a VR simulation to explore a reconstructed accident scene, helping them visualize the events and make more informed decisions.

Increased Efficiency and Cost Savings

By reducing the need for physical travel and minimizing the time required for certain legal processes, VR and AR can increase efficiency and reduce costs.

Example: A law firm uses AR to conduct remote consultations with clients, saving time and travel expenses while still providing high-quality legal services.

Enhanced Training Opportunities

VR and AR offer innovative training solutions that allow legal professionals to practice their skills in realistic scenarios without the risks associated with real-world practice.

Example: Law students use VR to simulate courtroom trials, gaining valuable experience and feedback in a controlled environment.

Greater Accessibility

These technologies can make legal services more accessible to individuals who face barriers such as financial constraints or geographical distances.

Example: A rural community uses VR to connect with legal professionals and access legal services that would otherwise be unavailable due to their remote location.

Challenges and Limitations

High Costs and Accessibility

The cost of VR and AR technology can be prohibitive, limiting its accessibility to those who can afford it. Additionally, the need for specialized equipment and technical expertise can create barriers to widespread adoption.

Example: A small law firm may struggle to invest in VR equipment and training for their staff due to budget constraints.

Technical Issues and User Discomfort

Technical issues such as motion sickness, disorientation, and sensory overload can affect users' comfort and ability to use VR and AR effectively. Additionally, people with certain mental health conditions may find these technologies challenging to use.

Example: A lawyer experiences motion sickness during a VR simulation, limiting their ability to use the technology for extended periods.

Ethical and Legal Concerns

The use of VR and AR raises ethical and legal concerns, such as privacy, security, and the potential for misuse. There is also a need to establish regulations and guidelines to ensure responsible and ethical use of these technologies.

Example: A legal firm must ensure that client data used in VR simulations is secure and complies with data protection regulations to prevent privacy breaches.

Practical Examples

Example 1: VR Training for Law Enforcement

Scenario: A police academy wants to improve its training program by providing realistic scenarios for cadets.

Traditional Approach: Training is conducted through classroom lectures and limited role-playing exercises.

VR Solution: The academy uses VR simulators to create immersive training scenarios, such as traffic stops, domestic disputes, and active shooter situations.

Outcome: Cadets receive hands-on training in realistic environments, improving their decision-making and response skills.

Example 2: AR for Crime Scene Analysis

Scenario: Investigators need to analyze a complex crime scene with multiple pieces of evidence.

Traditional Approach: Investigators physically visit the crime scene and manually document evidence, which can be time-consuming and prone to errors.

AR Solution: Investigators use AR glasses to overlay digital information onto the crime scene, providing real-time data and enhancing their analysis.

Outcome: The investigation is more efficient and accurate, with investigators able to visualize and document evidence more effectively.

Example 3: VR for Witness Preparation

Scenario: A lawyer needs to prepare a witness for an upcoming trial.

Traditional Approach: The lawyer conducts multiple in-person meetings with the witness to practice their testimony.

VR Solution: The lawyer uses VR to create a virtual courtroom, allowing the witness to practice their testimony in a realistic setting.

Outcome: The witness feels more confident and prepared for the trial, having practiced in an environment that closely resembles the actual courtroom.

Conclusion

Virtual and augmented reality technologies offer significant potential to transform the legal industry by enhancing training, improving evidence presentation, and increasing accessibility. While there are challenges and limitations to their widespread adoption, the benefits of VR and AR in law are substantial. By understanding and leveraging these technologies, legal professionals can provide more effective and efficient services, ultimately improving the delivery of justice.

BLOCKCHAIN AND SMART CONTRACTS PART 1: FUNDAMENTALS AND LEGAL APPLICATIONS

Introduction to Blockchain Technology

Blockchain technology is often described as a revolutionary innovation that has the potential to transform various industries, including law. At its core, blockchain is a decentralized, digital ledger that records transactions across multiple computers in such a way that the registered transactions cannot be altered retroactively. This chapter will introduce you to the fundamentals of blockchain technology, its mechanics, potential uses in the legal sector, and the concept of smart contracts. By the end of this chapter, you will have a foundational understanding of blockchain and its applications in law.

Understanding Blockchain Technology

What is Blockchain?

Blockchain technology can be thought of as a highly secure and transparent digital ledger. It consists of a chain of blocks, each containing a list of transactions. These blocks are linked together using cryptographic hashes, ensuring the integrity and immutability of the data.

Example: Imagine a digital ledger used by multiple parties in a real estate transaction. Every time a property changes hands, a new transaction is added to the blockchain, creating a permanent and unchangeable record of ownership.

The Mechanics of Blockchain

1. **Digital Signatures**: Transactions on a blockchain are initiated by users creating digital signatures, which verify their identity and ownership of the assets being transacted.
2. **Broadcasting Transactions**: Once a transaction is created, it is broadcast to a network of nodes (computers) that maintain a copy of the blockchain.
3. **Validation**: Nodes validate the transaction to ensure it is legitimate and adheres to the consensus rules of the network.
4. **Creating Blocks**: Validated transactions are bundled into a block.
5. **Consensus Protocol**: Nodes use a consensus protocol to agree on the validity of the block. Common protocols include Proof of Work (PoW) and Proof of Stake (PoS).

6. **Adding to the Blockchain**: Once validated, the block is added to the blockchain, becoming a part of the permanent and unalterable ledger.

Example: In a cryptocurrency network like Bitcoin, transactions are validated by miners who solve complex mathematical puzzles (Proof of Work) to add new blocks to the blockchain.

Key Components of Blockchain

- **Block**: A block is a list of transactions recorded over a certain period. Each block contains a unique digital fingerprint (hash) that links it to the previous block.
- **Chain**: The sequence of blocks that have been added to the blockchain over time.
- **Cryptographic Hash Function**: A security algorithm that generates a unique string of bytes from data records of any length, ensuring data integrity and immutability.
- **Node**: A computer or device connected to the blockchain network, participating in transaction validation, processing, and storage.

Example: A block in a blockchain might contain transactions related to the transfer of digital assets, with each transaction recorded and linked to previous transactions through cryptographic hashes.

Applications of Blockchain in Law

1. Identity Verification

Blockchain can improve the efficiency and security of identity verification processes by providing a decentralized and immutable ledger of identity information.

Example: Governments can use blockchain to maintain birth registrations, passport information, and other identity records, ensuring that the information is secure and easily verifiable.

2. Asset Management

Blockchain can create secure and transparent records of ownership and transactions for various assets, such as real estate, artwork, or financial instruments.

Example: A blockchain-based land registry can provide real-time title records, making property transactions more efficient and secure.

3. Supply Chain Transparency

Blockchain can be used to track the movement of goods and materials through a supply chain, providing transparency and accountability, and helping to prevent fraud and counterfeiting.

Example: A company can use blockchain to track the origin and journey of products, ensuring authenticity and reducing the risk of counterfeit goods entering the market.

4. Intellectual Property Protection

Blockchain can provide evidence of creation, first use, and rights management, making it easier for lawyers to track distribution and prevent copyright infringement.

Example: An artist registers their work on a blockchain, creating a timestamped and immutable record of their intellectual property, which can be used to prove ownership and rights in case of disputes.

5. Contract Management

Blockchain can facilitate the creation of self-executing smart contracts that automatically execute when certain conditions are met, reducing the need for intermediaries and streamlining the contract execution process.

Example: A smart contract can be used in a real estate transaction to automatically transfer ownership and funds once all conditions are satisfied, ensuring a secure and efficient process.

Introduction to Smart Contracts

What is a Smart Contract?

A smart contract is a self-executing contract with the terms of the agreement directly written into code. Smart contracts automatically enforce and execute the terms of the contract when predefined conditions are met, reducing the need for intermediaries and increasing efficiency.

Example: In a crowdfunding campaign, a smart contract can automatically release funds to the project creator once the funding goal is met, or refund contributors if the goal is not achieved by a certain deadline.

How Smart Contracts Work

1. **Coding the Contract**: The terms and conditions of the contract are coded into a smart contract using a programming language such as Solidity (used on the Ethereum blockchain).
2. **Deployment**: The smart contract is deployed to a blockchain, becoming a part of the decentralized network.
3. **Execution**: When predefined conditions are met, the smart contract automatically executes the agreed-upon actions, such as transferring funds or issuing a digital asset.

Example: A rental agreement could be coded into a smart contract, where the tenant's payment automatically triggers access to the rental property, eliminating the need for manual intervention by landlords or property managers.

Benefits of Smart Contracts

Efficiency and Speed

Smart contracts execute transactions automatically, reducing the time and effort required for manual processing and eliminating delays associated with traditional contract execution.

Example: A business-to-business transaction can be completed instantly using a smart contract, as opposed to waiting days or weeks for traditional bank transfers and contract reviews.

Transparency and Trust

The terms of smart contracts are visible and immutable on the blockchain, providing transparency and building trust among parties.

Example: In a supply chain agreement, all parties can see the terms and conditions of the smart contract, ensuring transparency and reducing disputes.

Cost Savings

Smart contracts eliminate the need for intermediaries, such as lawyers, brokers, or escrow services, reducing costs associated with contract execution and management.

Example: A freelancer uses a smart contract to receive payment for services upon project completion, eliminating the need for an escrow service and reducing transaction fees.

Security and Reliability

Smart contracts are secured by the blockchain's cryptographic algorithms, making them tamper-proof and reliable.

Example: A financial institution uses smart contracts for automated loan processing, ensuring secure and accurate execution of loan agreements.

Practical Examples of Blockchain and Smart Contracts

Example 1: Real Estate Transactions

Scenario: A buyer and seller are engaged in a real estate transaction.

Traditional Approach: The process involves multiple intermediaries, including real estate agents, lawyers, and escrow services, leading to high costs and delays.

Blockchain Solution: The transaction is executed using a smart contract on a blockchain. Once the buyer transfers the payment, the smart contract automatically transfers the property title to the buyer.

Outcome: The transaction is completed quickly, securely, and at a lower cost, without the need for intermediaries.

Example 2: Intellectual Property Protection

Scenario: An artist wants to protect their digital artwork and manage its distribution rights.

Traditional Approach: The artist registers their work with copyright offices and relies on legal mechanisms to enforce their rights, which can be time-consuming and costly.

Blockchain Solution: The artist registers their artwork on a blockchain, creating an immutable and timestamped record of ownership. Smart contracts are used to manage the sale and licensing of the artwork.

Outcome: The artist can easily prove ownership, manage rights, and receive payments automatically, reducing the risk of infringement and ensuring fair compensation.

Example 3: Supply Chain Management

Scenario: A company wants to ensure the authenticity and traceability of products in its supply chain.

Traditional Approach: The company uses paper-based records and manual tracking systems, which are prone to errors and fraud.

Blockchain Solution: The company uses blockchain to track the movement of goods through the supply chain, with each transaction recorded on an immutable ledger.

Outcome: The company can verify the authenticity of products, reduce fraud, and improve efficiency in the supply chain.

Conclusion

Blockchain and smart contracts are transformative technologies with the potential to revolutionize various aspects of the legal industry. By providing secure, transparent, and efficient solutions, these technologies can enhance the way legal transactions are conducted and managed. In the next part of this chapter, we will delve deeper into more advanced applications and explore how these technologies are being integrated into the legal ecosystem.

BLOCKCHAIN AND SMART CONTRACTS PART 2: ADVANCED APPLICATIONS IN LEGAL PRACTICE

Introduction to Advanced Applications and Challenges

In the first part of this chapter, we explored the basics of blockchain technology and smart contracts, including their key components, benefits, and practical examples. In this second part, we will delve deeper into the advanced applications of blockchain and smart contracts in various legal contexts, examine the implications of their use, and address the challenges and limitations that come with integrating these technologies into the legal industry. By the end of this chapter, you will have a comprehensive understanding of how blockchain and smart contracts can revolutionize the legal field and the hurdles that must be overcome to achieve their full potential.

Advanced Applications of Blockchain and Smart Contracts

Real Estate Transactions

Blockchain and smart contracts can streamline and secure real estate transactions by automating the process of transferring property ownership, reducing the need for intermediaries, and ensuring transparency.

Example: A property sale is facilitated by a smart contract that automatically transfers the deed to the buyer and the payment to the seller once all conditions are met, such as inspection approvals and financing.

Intellectual Property Management

Blockchain can provide a decentralized and immutable ledger for managing intellectual property rights, ensuring that creators can prove ownership and track the use of their works.

Example: A musician registers their songs on a blockchain platform, which records each time the song is played or licensed, automatically distributing royalties according to pre-set terms in a smart contract.

Government and Public Services

Blockchain and smart contracts can increase transparency and efficiency in government operations, such as voting systems, public records management, and social services.

Example: In a government election, a blockchain-based voting system ensures the integrity of the voting process by securely recording each vote and making the results publicly verifiable.

Healthcare and Medical Records

Blockchain technology can provide a secure and interoperable system for managing medical records, ensuring patient data is accessible to authorized healthcare providers while maintaining privacy and security.

Example: A patient's medical history is stored on a blockchain, allowing doctors and hospitals to access up-to-date information, reducing errors and improving the quality of care.

Supply Chain Management

Blockchain can enhance transparency and accountability in supply chains by providing a tamper-proof record of the journey of goods from origin to consumer.

Example: A company uses blockchain to track the production and shipping of its products, ensuring authenticity and reducing the risk of counterfeit goods.

Implications and Challenges of Blockchain and Smart Contracts

Legal and Regulatory Framework

The integration of blockchain and smart contracts into the legal industry requires a supportive legal and regulatory framework that recognizes and enforces these technologies.

Example: Legislators need to develop laws that recognize the legality of smart contracts and provide guidelines for their use, ensuring they are enforceable in court.

Integration with Existing Systems

Integrating blockchain technology with existing legal and business systems can be challenging, requiring significant investment in infrastructure and training.

Example: A law firm must update its case management and document storage systems to incorporate blockchain technology, ensuring seamless operation and data integrity.

Technical Expertise

The successful implementation of blockchain and smart contracts requires technical expertise, which can be a barrier for legal professionals who are not familiar with these technologies.

Example: Legal professionals need to acquire knowledge and skills in blockchain programming languages, such as Solidity, to effectively create and manage smart contracts.

Privacy and Security Concerns

While blockchain offers enhanced security, it also raises privacy concerns, especially when dealing with sensitive legal and personal data.

Example: Blockchain systems must be designed to protect personal information, complying with data protection regulations and ensuring that sensitive data is accessible only to authorized parties.

Resistance to Change

The adoption of new technologies can face resistance from stakeholders who are accustomed to traditional methods and wary of change.

Example: Some legal professionals may be reluctant to adopt blockchain and smart contracts due to concerns about their reliability, complexity, and impact on their practice.

Practical Examples of Overcoming Challenges

Example 1: Legal Framework Development

Scenario: A government aims to support the use of smart contracts in commercial transactions.

Solution: The government enacts legislation that recognizes the legal validity of smart contracts, provides guidelines for their use, and ensures they are enforceable in court.

Outcome: Businesses can confidently use smart contracts for commercial transactions, knowing they are supported by a clear legal framework.

Example 2: Integration with Existing Systems

Scenario: A law firm wants to integrate blockchain technology into its case management system.

Solution: The firm collaborates with a blockchain technology provider to develop a custom solution that integrates blockchain with its existing systems, providing training for staff to ensure smooth adoption.

Outcome: The firm successfully integrates blockchain technology, improving data security and operational efficiency.

Example 3: Addressing Privacy Concerns

Scenario: A healthcare provider wants to use blockchain for managing patient records but is concerned about privacy.

Solution: The provider implements a private blockchain that uses encryption and access controls to protect patient data, ensuring compliance with data protection regulations.

Outcome: Patient records are securely managed on the blockchain, with access restricted to authorized healthcare providers.

Example 4: Training and Education

Scenario: Legal professionals need to acquire skills in blockchain and smart contracts to meet client demands.

Solution: Law schools and professional organizations offer training programs and certifications in blockchain technology, providing legal professionals with the knowledge and skills they need.

Outcome: Legal professionals are equipped to advise clients on blockchain and smart contracts, expanding their practice and meeting market demand.

Conclusion

Blockchain and smart contracts hold immense potential to transform the legal industry by increasing efficiency, security, and transparency. However, realizing this potential requires addressing significant challenges, including developing a supportive legal framework, integrating with existing systems, acquiring technical expertise, and addressing privacy concerns. By overcoming these hurdles, legal professionals can leverage blockchain technology to provide more effective and innovative services to their clients.

KEY ETHICAL ISSUES IN LEGAL TECH AND ARTIFICIAL INTELLIGENCE (AI): AN IN-DEPTH LOOK

Introduction to Ethics in Legal Tech

As legal technology and artificial intelligence (AI) become integral parts of the legal industry, ensuring their ethical use is paramount. The adoption of these technologies raises numerous ethical considerations that must be addressed to uphold the core values of the legal profession, protect client interests, and promote justice. This chapter will explore the key ethical issues associated with legal tech and AI, providing practical examples and guidelines to help legal professionals navigate these challenges responsibly.

Key Ethical Considerations in Legal Tech

Data Protection and Privacy

The use of legal technology often involves handling sensitive client data. Ensuring the protection and confidentiality of this data is crucial to maintaining client trust and meeting ethical obligations.

Example: A law firm uses a cloud-based legal management system to store client information. To protect this data, the firm implements robust encryption, access controls, and regular security audits.

Bias and Fairness

Algorithms and machine learning models used in legal tech can inadvertently learn and perpetuate biases present in their training data, leading to unfair outcomes. Ensuring fairness and mitigating bias in AI systems is essential.

Example: A predictive policing tool is found to disproportionately target minority communities due to biased historical data. The developers address this by retraining the model with diverse and representative data and regularly auditing its outcomes for fairness.

Transparency and Accountability

Legal tech companies must be transparent about how their technologies work, what data they collect, and how they influence legal decisions. This transparency ensures that legal professionals and clients can make informed decisions about using these technologies.

Example: An AI-based legal research tool provides detailed explanations of how it generates its recommendations, including the sources of its data and the logic behind its algorithms, enabling users to understand and trust its outputs.

Accessibility and Inclusivity

Legal technology should be designed to be accessible and affordable to a wide range of users, including those with disabilities. This promotes equal access to justice and prevents the creation of new barriers.

Example: A legal chatbot is designed with assistive technologies such as text-to-speech and screen reader compatibility, ensuring that users with visual impairments can fully utilize its services.

Professional Responsibility

Legal professionals must ensure that the use of technology does not compromise their professional responsibilities, including competence, confidentiality, and the duty to supervise.

Example: A lawyer uses AI to draft a contract but carefully reviews and edits the document to ensure it meets all legal requirements and serves the client's best interests.

Ethical Challenges and Case Studies

Case Study 1: Data Breach in a Legal Tech Firm

Scenario: A legal tech firm experiences a data breach, compromising sensitive client information.

Ethical Issues: The breach raises concerns about data protection, client confidentiality, and the firm's adherence to ethical standards.

Response: The firm takes immediate steps to mitigate the breach, including notifying affected clients, enhancing security measures, and providing transparency about the incident. The firm also reviews and updates its data protection policies to prevent future breaches.

Outcome: By addressing the breach responsibly and transparently, the firm restores client trust and reinforces its commitment to ethical standards.

Case Study 2: Bias in AI-Powered Legal Tools

Scenario: An AI tool used for sentencing recommendations is found to have a bias against minority groups.

Ethical Issues: The biased outcomes result in unfair sentencing, violating principles of justice and equality.

Response: The developers retrain the AI model using a more diverse dataset, implement regular bias audits, and engage with ethicists and community representatives to ensure fairness.

Outcome: The improved AI tool provides fairer recommendations, and the developers' proactive approach enhances the tool's credibility and ethical standing.

Case Study 3: Transparency in AI Legal Research Tools

Scenario: A law firm uses an AI-powered research tool that does not disclose its data sources or algorithms.

Ethical Issues: The lack of transparency makes it difficult for lawyers to assess the tool's reliability and trustworthiness.

Response: The law firm demands greater transparency from the tool's developers and opts to use tools that provide clear explanations of their processes.

Outcome: The firm ensures that it uses reliable and transparent technology, maintaining its commitment to ethical practice and informed decision-making.

Guidelines for Ethical Use of Legal Tech and AI

Develop Clear Policies

Create comprehensive policies regarding data privacy, security, and confidentiality. Ensure these policies comply with legal and ethical standards.

Example: A law firm implements a data privacy policy that outlines how client data is collected, stored, and protected, ensuring compliance with data protection regulations.

Ensure Transparency

Legal tech companies should provide clear and comprehensive disclosures about how their products work, including any limitations and risks.

Example: A developer of an AI legal assistant includes a detailed user guide that explains how the AI generates its responses, potential limitations, and how to interpret its outputs responsibly.

Address Bias and Fairness

Regularly audit AI systems for bias and take corrective actions to ensure fairness and justice in their outputs.

Example: A legal analytics firm conducts quarterly audits of its predictive models to identify and correct any biases, ensuring fair and unbiased outcomes.

Enhance Accessibility

Design legal technology to be inclusive and accessible to all users, including those with disabilities.

Example: A legal tech company develops its platform with accessibility features such as keyboard navigation, screen reader compatibility, and customizable text sizes to ensure all users can access its services.

Promote Professional Responsibility

Ensure that the use of technology does not compromise legal professionals' responsibilities, such as competence and confidentiality.

Example: A legal professional uses AI to assist with document review but maintains oversight and responsibility for the final review, ensuring that the technology complements rather than replaces their expertise.

Conclusion

Ethics in legal tech and AI is a critical consideration that must be addressed to ensure the responsible and fair use of these technologies. By adhering to ethical guidelines and addressing challenges such as data protection, bias, transparency, accessibility, and professional responsibility, legal professionals can leverage technology to enhance their practice while upholding the core values of the legal profession. In the next chapter, we will explore future trends in legal tech and AI, providing insights into the innovations that are set to shape the legal industry.

PROTECTING CLIENT INFORMATION: PRIVACY, CONFIDENTIALITY, AND CYBERSECURITY IN LAW

Introduction

In the digital age, legal technology and artificial intelligence have introduced new challenges related to privacy, confidentiality, cybersecurity, and the unauthorized practice of law (UPL). As these technologies become increasingly integrated into legal practice, it is crucial for legal professionals and tech companies to understand and address these issues to protect client information, uphold ethical standards, and comply with regulations. This chapter provides an in-depth exploration of these critical topics, complete with practical examples to help beginners navigate these complex areas.

Privacy and Confidentiality in Legal Tech

Privacy

Privacy refers to an individual's right to control access to their personal information and protect it from public scrutiny. In the legal context, privacy is essential for safeguarding sensitive client data and maintaining trust.

Example: A law firm ensures that all client communications are encrypted and access to case files is restricted to authorized personnel only, protecting clients' personal and sensitive information.

Confidentiality

Confidentiality is a legal duty to keep sensitive information entrusted to legal professionals secret. This obligation is fundamental to the attorney-client relationship and critical for protecting client rights and interests.

Example: An attorney uses a secure client portal to share confidential documents, ensuring that only the client can access the information.

Threats to Privacy and Confidentiality

Hacking

Hacking involves unauthorized access to computer systems, often for financial gain or personal motives. Hackers can target legal tech systems to steal sensitive information.

Example: A hacker gains access to a law firm's network, stealing confidential client information and causing significant financial and reputational damage.

Data Breaches

A data breach occurs when sensitive information is accessed, exposed, or lost due to malicious attacks, employee errors, or third-party vulnerabilities.

Example: An employee inadvertently sends confidential client data to the wrong email address, resulting in a data breach.

Phishing

Phishing attacks deceive individuals into revealing sensitive information by impersonating a trustworthy source, typically via email or other digital communication channels.

Example: A lawyer receives a phishing email that appears to be from a trusted client, prompting them to click a malicious link that compromises their login credentials.

Social Engineering

Social engineering involves manipulating individuals into divulging sensitive information or performing actions that are not in their best interests, often by exploiting human emotions or biases.

Example: A cybercriminal impersonates an IT support staff member and convinces a legal assistant to reveal their password.

Cybersecurity in Legal Tech

Importance of Cybersecurity

Cybersecurity is crucial for protecting sensitive legal data and information from cyberattacks and data breaches. Legal tech companies and law firms must implement robust measures to safeguard their systems and data.

Example: A law firm implements multi-factor authentication and regular security assessments to protect its digital infrastructure from cyber threats.

Key Cybersecurity Measures

Data Encryption

Encrypting data in transit and at rest ensures that sensitive information is protected from unauthorized access.

Example: A legal tech platform encrypts all client data stored on its servers and during transmission to ensure confidentiality.

Access Control

Restricting access to sensitive data to authorized personnel and implementing strong authentication measures, such as multi-factor authentication, helps prevent unauthorized access.

Example: A legal department uses role-based access control to limit access to case files based on employees' roles and responsibilities.

Security Monitoring

Continuous security monitoring helps detect and respond to security incidents quickly. This includes using firewalls, intrusion detection systems, and regular security audits.

Example: A legal tech company uses intrusion detection systems to monitor network traffic for unusual activities and respond to potential threats.

Data Backup and Recovery

Regular data backups and a well-defined recovery strategy ensure that sensitive data can be restored in case of data loss or corruption.

Example: A law firm schedules daily backups of all client data and tests its recovery system monthly to ensure data integrity and availability.

Employee Training

Training employees on cybersecurity best practices, including password management, phishing awareness, and secure data handling, helps prevent security incidents caused by human error.

Example: A legal tech company conducts quarterly cybersecurity training sessions for all staff, emphasizing the importance of protecting client information.

Unauthorized Practice of Law (UPL)

Definition and Importance

Unauthorized practice of law refers to the provision of legal services by individuals or organizations without a license to practice law. This includes offering legal advice, drafting legal documents, and representing clients in court.

Example: A non-lawyer offers legal advice and drafts contracts for clients, which constitutes unauthorized practice of law and can lead to legal penalties.

UPL Laws and Regulations

Each jurisdiction has specific laws and standards governing the unauthorized practice of law to protect the public from subpar or dishonest legal services.

Example: A technology company providing automated legal document services ensures that all legal advice is reviewed and provided by licensed attorneys to comply with UPL regulations.

Technology and UPL

Legal tech companies must carefully navigate UPL laws when offering automated legal services or operating legal marketplaces. They should provide clear disclaimers and ensure that legal documents and advice are provided by licensed attorneys.

Example: A legal tech platform includes disclaimers that it is not a law firm and ensures that all legal document templates are created and reviewed by licensed attorneys.

Case Studies

Case Study 1: Data Breach in a Legal Tech Firm

Scenario: A legal tech firm experiences a data breach, compromising sensitive client information.

Response: The firm notifies affected clients, enhances security measures, and provides transparency about the incident. They review and update their data protection policies to prevent future breaches.

Outcome: The firm restores client trust by addressing the breach responsibly and transparently.

Case Study 2: Bias in AI-Powered Legal Tools

Scenario: An AI tool used for sentencing recommendations is found to have a bias against minority groups.

Response: The developers retrain the AI model with diverse data, implement regular bias audits, and engage ethicists to ensure fairness.

Outcome: The improved AI tool provides fairer recommendations, enhancing its credibility and ethical standing.

Case Study 3: UPL Concerns in a Legal Tech Company

Scenario: A legal tech company offers automated legal document services and faces allegations of UPL.

Response: The company ensures that all legal documents are reviewed by licensed attorneys and includes clear disclaimers about its services.

Outcome: The company complies with UPL laws and provides reliable legal services while avoiding legal penalties.

Conclusion

Addressing privacy, confidentiality, cybersecurity, and unauthorized practice of law is crucial for the ethical and legal use of technology in the legal industry. By implementing robust security measures, complying with regulations, and maintaining high ethical standards, legal professionals and tech companies can protect client information, uphold public trust, and navigate the complexities of modern legal practice.

REAL-WORLD LEGAL CHALLENGES AND LESSONS LEARNED FROM: PRIVACY, CYBERSECURITY, AND UNAUTHORIZED PRACTICE

Introduction

In the rapidly evolving landscape of legal technology and artificial intelligence, the professional and ethical implications of these advancements are profound. This chapter will delve into real-world case studies that highlight the challenges and lessons learned from privacy breaches, cybersecurity attacks, and issues related to the unauthorized practice of law. These examples will provide valuable insights for legal professionals, helping them navigate the complexities of ethical and professional standards in a tech-driven world.

Case Study 1: Clearview AI - Privacy and Data Scraping

Background

Clearview AI is a legal technology company that provides facial recognition services to law enforcement agencies. The company faced significant backlash when it was discovered that it had scraped images from social media platforms without individuals' consent and provided these to law enforcement agencies without proper oversight.

Ethical and Professional Issues

- **Privacy Violations**: Clearview AI collected personal images without user consent, violating privacy laws and ethical standards.
- **Lack of Transparency**: The company's lack of transparency about data collection methods raised significant ethical concerns.
- **Regulatory Actions**: The company faced lawsuits and regulatory actions, including a lawsuit filed by the ACLU and state attorney generals.

Response and Outcome

Clearview AI implemented a new privacy policy, limiting its use to law enforcement agencies and requiring them to sign contracts before gaining access to the software. This case highlights the need for clear guidelines on data collection, consent, and transparency in legal technology.

Example: Clearview AI's experience underscores the importance of obtaining explicit consent from individuals before collecting and using their data. Legal tech companies must ensure that their data practices comply with privacy laws and ethical standards to maintain public trust and avoid legal repercussions.

Case Study 2: The Panama Papers - Confidentiality Breach

Background

In 2016, a massive leak of documents known as the Panama Papers revealed that the law firm Mossack Fonseca had helped wealthy clients establish offshore companies to avoid taxes. The leak exposed confidential client information and led to a significant loss of trust.

Ethical and Professional Issues

- **Client Confidentiality**: The breach was a significant violation of client confidentiality, a core ethical obligation for legal professionals.
- **Data Security**: The leak highlighted critical weaknesses in the firm's data security practices.
- **Reputational Damage**: The firm faced numerous lawsuits and investigations, ultimately shutting down operations in several countries.

Lessons Learned

This case emphasized the need for law firms to implement robust data security measures, including regular software updates, restricted access to sensitive data, and thorough audits. Ensuring the separation of services and isolating data can also help mitigate the impact of potential breaches.

Example: Mossack Fonseca's failure to protect client data demonstrates the critical importance of maintaining strong cybersecurity practices. Law firms must regularly review and update their security protocols to safeguard client information and uphold their ethical responsibilities.

Case Study 3: Goodwin Procter - Third-Party Vendor Breach

Background

In 2019, the law firm Goodwin Procter experienced a data breach due to a hack on a third-party vendor that handled their large file transfers. This incident highlighted the risks associated with outsourcing services to third parties.

Ethical and Professional Issues

- **Vendor Management**: Outsourcing to third-party vendors can introduce vulnerabilities, making it essential to ensure that these vendors adhere to stringent security standards.
- **Data Protection**: The breach raised concerns about the firm's ability to protect sensitive client data.

Response and Outcome

Goodwin Procter enhanced its third-party vendor management practices, ensuring that all vendors comply with their data security requirements. This case underscores the importance of vetting third-party vendors and implementing strict data protection policies.

Example: Law firms must conduct thorough due diligence when selecting third-party vendors and continuously monitor their security practices to prevent data breaches and protect client information.

Case Study 4: LegalZoom - Unauthorized Practice of Law

Background

LegalZoom, an online legal document preparation service, faced accusations of unauthorized practice of law. Some legal professionals argued that LegalZoom's services crossed the line into providing legal advice, which requires a license to practice law.

Ethical and Professional Issues

- **Unauthorized Practice of Law (UPL)**: Offering legal advice without a license is illegal and undermines the professional standards of the legal industry.
- **Consumer Protection**: Clients may receive inaccurate or incomplete legal advice from unlicensed providers, potentially leading to adverse outcomes.

Response and Outcome

LegalZoom settled the dispute by making changes to its business practices and paying costs related to the investigation. The company also included disclaimers on its website to clarify that it is not a substitute for a licensed attorney.

Example: Legal tech companies must ensure that their services do not constitute unauthorized practice of law. Including clear disclaimers and working with licensed attorneys can help mitigate legal risks and protect consumers.

Case Study 5: Seyfarth Shaw - Ransomware Attack

Background

Seyfarth Shaw, a large US law firm, suffered a ransomware attack that impacted its energy infrastructure. The firm had to temporarily shut down its systems to prevent the spread of malware and ensure data security.

Ethical and Professional Issues

- **Cybersecurity Preparedness**: The attack highlighted the need for law firms to have robust cybersecurity measures in place.
- **Business Continuity**: Ensuring that critical services remain operational during a cyberattack is essential for maintaining client trust and meeting professional obligations.

Response and Outcome

Seyfarth Shaw implemented enhanced cybersecurity protocols and developed a comprehensive incident response plan to address future threats. This case underscores the importance of preparedness and quick response in maintaining data security and client trust.

Example: Law firms must regularly update their cybersecurity measures and have well-defined incident response plans to address potential cyber threats effectively.

Conclusion

These case studies illustrate the complex ethical and professional challenges that arise in the intersection of legal technology and practice. By learning from these real-world examples, legal professionals can better navigate the ethical landscape, implement robust security measures, and ensure compliance with legal standards. Addressing these issues proactively helps maintain public trust, protect client interests, and uphold the integrity of the legal profession.

ADAPTING TO CHANGE: THE IMPACT OF TECHNOLOGY ON LEGAL CAREERS

Introduction

Technology is transforming the legal profession, reshaping job roles, career paths, and the skills required to succeed. As the legal industry evolves, professionals must adapt to stay relevant and leverage new opportunities created by technological advancements. This chapter explores the impact of technology on legal jobs and careers, providing detailed insights and practical examples to help beginners understand and navigate this dynamic landscape.

The Evolving Legal Job Market

Traditional vs. Modern Legal Careers

Traditionally, aspiring lawyers followed a straightforward career path: attending law school, passing the bar exam, and practicing law until retirement. However, this path is no longer the norm as technology reshapes the legal profession, introducing new roles and career opportunities.

Example: A lawyer specializing in litigation may now transition to a legal tech consultant, helping firms implement and optimize AI-driven legal research tools.

Automation and Job Displacement

The integration of technology and automation in the legal industry has led to the displacement of certain job functions, particularly those involving routine administrative tasks. While this reduces opportunities for some traditional roles, it also creates new ones focused on strategic, value-adding tasks.

Example: Paralegals traditionally tasked with document review may now oversee AI-powered review systems, focusing on higher-level analysis and quality control.

Emerging Roles in Legal Tech

Legal Technologists

Legal technologists bridge the gap between law and technology, developing and managing legal tech solutions to improve efficiency and service delivery. They possess both legal knowledge and technical skills, making them invaluable in modern legal practice.

Example: A legal technologist might develop a blockchain-based contract management system, ensuring secure and transparent transactions for clients.

Legal Operations Professionals

Legal operations professionals focus on optimizing the business and operational aspects of legal practice. They implement process improvements, manage budgets, and leverage technology to enhance productivity and client service.

Example: A legal operations manager might streamline case management by integrating an AI-powered legal analytics platform, reducing costs and improving case outcomes.

Project Managers

Project managers in law oversee complex legal projects, ensuring they are completed on time, within budget, and to the client's satisfaction. They coordinate resources, manage timelines, and use technology to facilitate collaboration.

Example: A project manager might use a legal project management tool to coordinate a large-scale e-discovery project, tracking progress and managing resources effectively.

Alternative Legal Service Providers (ALSPs)

ALSPs offer specialized legal services such as document review, contract management, and e-discovery, often using standardized processes and automation. They hire a mix of lawyers, legal technologists, analysts, and project managers.

Example: An ALSP specializing in e-discovery might use advanced analytics to quickly identify relevant documents, reducing time and costs for their clients.

Skills for the Modern Legal Professional

Technological Proficiency

Understanding and utilizing legal technology is essential for modern legal professionals. This includes familiarity with AI, blockchain, data analytics, and other emerging technologies.

Example: A lawyer proficient in AI might use predictive analytics to assess the likely outcome of a case, providing clients with data-driven advice.

Client Engagement

Exceptional client service is increasingly important in a competitive legal market. Lawyers who can communicate effectively, empathize with clients, and understand their needs are in high demand.

Example: A client-focused lawyer might use a CRM system to track client interactions and tailor their services to meet individual client needs.

Project Management

Effective project management skills are vital for coordinating complex legal tasks, managing resources, and ensuring timely delivery of services.

Example: A lawyer with strong project management skills might lead a cross-functional team to develop a new legal tech product, ensuring it meets client requirements and regulatory standards.

Continuous Learning

The rapid pace of technological change requires legal professionals to engage in continuous learning and upskilling. This includes staying updated on the latest trends and acquiring new skills in technology, people management, and process optimization.

Example: A lawyer might attend workshops on blockchain technology and its applications in law, enhancing their expertise and marketability.

Practical Examples of Career Adaptation

Example 1: Transitioning to Legal Tech Consulting

Scenario: A mid-career lawyer specializing in corporate law decides to transition to legal tech consulting.

Actions: The lawyer undertakes training in AI and legal tech solutions, gaining certification in relevant technologies. They join a consulting firm and help law firms implement AI-driven contract review systems.

Outcome: The lawyer leverages their legal expertise and new tech skills to provide valuable consulting services, enjoying a dynamic and fulfilling career.

Example 2: Embracing Legal Project Management

Scenario: A paralegal wants to enhance their career prospects by specializing in legal project management.

Actions: The paralegal enrolls in project management courses and gains certification. They start managing e-discovery projects, using project management software to track progress and resources.

Outcome: The paralegal's project management skills lead to increased responsibilities and career advancement, contributing to the firm's efficiency and client satisfaction.

Example 3: Joining an Alternative Legal Service Provider

Scenario: A recent law graduate is interested in working for an ALSP rather than a traditional law firm.

Actions: The graduate applies for positions at ALSPs, emphasizing their technical skills and willingness to work in innovative environments. They join an ALSP specializing in contract management, using automation tools to handle large volumes of contracts efficiently.

Outcome: The graduate gains valuable experience in a cutting-edge legal environment, with opportunities for rapid career growth and specialization.

Conclusion

Technology is reshaping the legal profession, creating new job roles and career opportunities while transforming existing ones. Legal professionals must adapt by acquiring new skills, embracing continuous learning, and leveraging technology to enhance their practice. By understanding and navigating the impact of technology on jobs and careers, legal professionals can secure successful and fulfilling futures in this dynamic field.

UNDERSTANDING I-SHAPED, T-SHAPED, AND DELTA-SHAPED PROFESSIONALS

Introduction

In the evolving landscape of the legal profession, the skill sets and expertise required for success have expanded significantly. The traditional "I-shaped" model of legal professionals, which emphasized deep specialization in one area of law, has given way to more versatile models such as the "T-shaped" and "Delta-shaped" professionals. These new models reflect the need for a broader range of skills, including technical proficiency, business acumen, and personal effectiveness. This chapter explores these models in detail, providing practical examples to help beginners understand the diverse skill sets required in modern legal practice.

The I-Shaped Legal Professional

Overview

The I-shaped legal professional represents the traditional model, characterized by deep expertise and specialization in a specific area of law. This model focuses on mastering legal principles, research, analysis, writing, and advocacy skills.

Example: A lawyer specializing in intellectual property law spends years developing in-depth knowledge and expertise in this field, handling complex IP litigation and advising clients on patent and trademark issues.

Strengths

- **Deep Expertise**: I-shaped professionals are highly knowledgeable in their area of specialization, providing expert advice and representation.
- **Focused Skill Development**: Their education and career development are concentrated on mastering specific legal principles and practices.

Limitations

- **Narrow Skill Set**: The emphasis on specialization can limit their ability to adapt to broader roles and responsibilities.
- **Client Expectations**: Modern clients demand a wider range of skills and interdisciplinary knowledge, which the I-shaped model may not fully address.

The T-Shaped Legal Professional

Overview

The T-shaped model builds upon the I-shaped model by combining deep legal expertise with a broad range of skills and knowledge in other areas. The vertical bar of the T represents the lawyer's deep expertise in their specific area of law, while the horizontal bar represents their ability to collaborate with professionals from other disciplines and draw on a wide range of skills outside of law.

Example: A corporate lawyer with deep expertise in mergers and acquisitions (M&A) also possesses strong skills in project management, data analytics, and financial analysis, allowing them to manage complex transactions more effectively.

Strengths

- **Versatility**: T-shaped professionals can apply their legal expertise in various contexts, collaborating effectively with other professionals.
- **Broader Skill Set**: They possess non-legal skills such as project management, technology, and finance, making them more valuable to clients and employers.

Limitations

- **Balancing Depth and Breadth**: Developing both deep expertise and a broad skill set can be challenging, requiring continuous learning and adaptation.

The Delta-Shaped Legal Professional

Overview

The Delta-shaped model, or the "Delta Lawyer," is an evolution of the T-shaped model that incorporates three dimensions of competencies: legal knowledge, business and operations, and personal effectiveness. This model ensures that lawyers develop a well-rounded skill set that adapts to the ever-changing legal landscape.

Example: A litigation lawyer not only excels in courtroom advocacy but also possesses strong business acumen and personal effectiveness skills such as emotional intelligence, communication, and relationship management.

Components

1. **Legal Knowledge**: Traditional legal skills such as legal writing, analysis, and research.
2. **Business and Operations**: Skills like project management, data analytics, and understanding of business processes.

3. **Personal Effectiveness**: Attributes like emotional intelligence, entrepreneurial mindset, and effective communication.

Strengths

- **Comprehensive Skill Set**: Delta-shaped professionals are well-rounded, capable of excelling in various aspects of legal practice.
- **Adaptability**: They can adapt to different roles and challenges, providing greater value to clients and organizations.

Limitations

- **Complex Development**: Achieving proficiency in all three dimensions requires significant effort and ongoing professional development.

Practical Examples

Example 1: Transitioning from I-Shaped to T-Shaped

Scenario: A criminal defense attorney specializing in trial advocacy decides to expand their skill set to meet the demands of modern legal practice.

Actions: The attorney takes courses in forensic technology, learns data analysis techniques, and collaborates with forensic experts to enhance their case preparation and presentation.

Outcome: The attorney becomes a T-shaped professional, providing more comprehensive defense strategies that incorporate forensic evidence and data analysis.

Example 2: Adopting the Delta Model in Corporate Law

Scenario: A corporate lawyer aims to become a Delta-shaped professional to better serve their clients.

Actions: The lawyer pursues an MBA to gain business and financial skills, attends workshops on emotional intelligence, and participates in leadership training programs.

Outcome: The lawyer enhances their legal expertise with business acumen and personal effectiveness skills, becoming a trusted advisor who can navigate complex corporate transactions and lead multidisciplinary teams.

Example 3: Enhancing Collaboration as a T-Shaped Legal Professional

Scenario: A family lawyer recognizes the need to collaborate more effectively with professionals from other disciplines, such as social workers and financial planners.

Actions: The lawyer builds knowledge in areas like family finance and child psychology, attends interdisciplinary conferences, and establishes networks with other professionals.

Outcome: The lawyer becomes a T-shaped professional, capable of providing holistic support to clients by integrating legal advice with insights from other fields.

Conclusion

The evolution from I-shaped to T-shaped and Delta-shaped models reflects the changing demands of the legal profession. Modern legal professionals must develop a diverse skill set that combines deep legal expertise with business acumen and personal effectiveness. By understanding these models and continuously adapting their skills, legal professionals can provide greater value to their clients and thrive in a dynamic legal landscape.

HOW TO DEVELOP A DIGITAL MINDSET FOR LEGAL SUCCESS

Introduction

In the fast-paced world of legal technology and artificial intelligence, developing a digital mindset is crucial for legal professionals to stay competitive and efficient. A digital mindset involves adopting attitudes and behaviors that embrace change, leverage technology, and create new possibilities. This chapter will guide you through the concept of a digital mindset, its importance, and how to cultivate it, with practical examples to illustrate the transformation from traditional to digital thinking.

Understanding the Digital Mindset

Definition

A digital mindset is a set of attitudes and behaviors that enable individuals and organizations to recognize the opportunities created by digital technologies, such as data, algorithms, and AI. It involves being adaptable, open to change, and continuously seeking to leverage technology to improve processes and outcomes.

Example: A traditional lawyer may rely on physical files and face-to-face meetings, while a lawyer with a digital mindset uses cloud-based document management and video conferencing to streamline their workflow and enhance client communication.

Key Components of a Digital Mindset

1. **Adaptability**: Being flexible and open to new ideas and technologies.
2. **Continuous Learning**: Staying updated on the latest technological advancements and upskilling regularly.
3. **Collaboration**: Working effectively with others, including those from different disciplines and backgrounds.
4. **Innovation**: Seeking out and implementing new ways to solve problems and improve processes.
5. **Data-Driven Decision Making**: Using data and analytics to inform decisions and strategies.

The Importance of a Digital Mindset

Staying Competitive

In the legal industry, clients increasingly expect efficient, technology-driven services. A digital mindset enables legal professionals to meet these expectations and stay competitive in a rapidly changing market.

Example: A law firm that adopts AI-powered legal research tools can provide faster and more accurate legal advice, giving it a competitive edge over firms that rely solely on traditional methods.

Enhancing Efficiency

Technology can streamline many legal processes, from document review to case management. A digital mindset helps professionals identify and leverage these technologies to improve efficiency and reduce costs.

Example: Using e-discovery software, a legal team can quickly analyze large volumes of documents, significantly reducing the time and cost associated with manual review.

Improving Client Service

Clients value transparency, speed, and accessibility. A digital mindset allows legal professionals to use technology to enhance client service and satisfaction.

Example: Implementing a client portal where clients can access their case information, communicate with their lawyer, and upload documents at any time improves client engagement and satisfaction.

Cultivating a Digital Mindset

Embracing Change

The first step in developing a digital mindset is to embrace change. This means being open to new technologies, processes, and ways of thinking.

Example: A senior partner at a law firm encourages the adoption of a new case management system, despite initial resistance from some team members, by highlighting the long-term benefits of improved efficiency and client service.

Continuous Learning and Upskilling

Staying current with technological advancements is crucial. Legal professionals should engage in continuous learning and upskilling to keep pace with changes in the industry.

Example: A lawyer enrolls in online courses on blockchain technology and its applications in law, enhancing their ability to advise clients on emerging legal issues.

Leveraging Technology

Identify and implement technologies that can improve your practice. This might include AI, machine learning, blockchain, and data analytics tools.

Example: A legal department implements an AI-powered contract analysis tool to automatically review and flag potential issues in contracts, saving time and reducing errors.

Encouraging Collaboration

Foster a culture of collaboration within your organization. Work with colleagues from different disciplines and backgrounds to leverage diverse perspectives and expertise.

Example: A law firm creates cross-functional teams that include IT specialists, data analysts, and legal professionals to develop innovative solutions for client needs.

Data-Driven Decision Making

Use data and analytics to inform your decisions and strategies. This approach can lead to more accurate and effective outcomes.

Example: A legal team uses data analytics to assess the likelihood of success in litigation cases, allowing them to advise clients more accurately on whether to settle or proceed to trial.

Practical Examples of Developing a Digital Mindset

Example 1: Adopting Cloud-Based Solutions

Scenario: A traditional law firm is struggling with the inefficiencies of paper-based document management.

Actions: The firm transitions to a cloud-based document management system, training staff on its use and emphasizing the benefits of accessibility, security, and collaboration.

Outcome: The firm experiences significant improvements in efficiency and client service, with lawyers able to access and share documents from anywhere, at any time.

Example 2: Implementing AI for Legal Research

Scenario: A legal research team spends countless hours manually sifting through case law and statutes.

Actions: The team adopts an AI-powered legal research tool that uses natural language processing to quickly identify relevant cases and statutes.

Outcome: The team reduces research time dramatically, allowing lawyers to focus on higher-value tasks and provide faster, more accurate legal advice.

Example 3: Enhancing Client Communication with Technology

Scenario: A law firm struggles with maintaining effective communication with clients, leading to dissatisfaction and lost business.

Actions: The firm implements a client portal and communication platform, enabling clients to access their case information, schedule appointments, and communicate with their lawyer online.

Outcome: Client satisfaction and engagement improve, leading to increased client retention and positive referrals.

Overcoming Resistance to a Digital Mindset

Identifying Barriers

Resistance to change can stem from various factors, including fear of the unknown, comfort with existing processes, and lack of understanding of new technologies.

Example: A lawyer accustomed to traditional methods may be hesitant to adopt new technology due to a lack of familiarity and fear of making mistakes.

Addressing Resistance

To overcome resistance, it is essential to provide education, demonstrate the benefits of new technologies, and create a supportive environment for change.

Example: A law firm offers training sessions and hands-on workshops to help staff become comfortable with new technology, highlighting success stories and tangible benefits.

Encouraging a Growth Mindset

Promote a growth mindset within your organization, encouraging continuous learning, experimentation, and acceptance of failure as part of the innovation process.

Example: Leadership at a law firm celebrates successes and learns from failures, fostering a culture where trying new things is encouraged and supported.

Conclusion

Developing a digital mindset is essential for legal professionals to thrive in today's technology-driven world. By embracing change, continuously learning, leveraging technology, fostering collaboration, and making data-driven decisions, legal professionals can enhance their efficiency, stay competitive, and provide superior client service. Cultivating a digital mindset requires effort and commitment, but the benefits are significant, positioning individuals and organizations for success in the evolving legal landscape.

HOW TO TRANSFORM YOURSELF INTO A DIGITAL LEGAL PROFESSIONAL

Introduction

In the rapidly evolving legal industry, becoming a digital legal professional is essential for staying competitive and providing efficient services. This chapter will guide you through the process of acquiring the skills, mindset, and tools necessary to thrive in a digital legal environment. By the end of this chapter, you will have a clear understanding of how to transform yourself into a proficient digital legal professional, with practical examples to help you apply these concepts effectively.

Understanding the Digital Legal Professional

What is a Digital Legal Professional?

A digital legal professional is someone who leverages technology to enhance their legal practice. This includes using digital tools for research, document management, client communication, and legal analytics. A digital legal professional is adaptable, continuously learning, and proficient in both legal and technological skills.

Example: A lawyer who uses AI-powered legal research tools to quickly find relevant case law and draft legal documents more efficiently.

Importance of Becoming a Digital Legal Professional

1. **Increased Efficiency**: Technology can automate routine tasks, allowing you to focus on higher-value work.
2. **Enhanced Client Service**: Digital tools enable better communication, faster response times, and more transparent processes.
3. **Competitive Advantage**: Being proficient in legal tech can set you apart from other professionals and attract tech-savvy clients.
4. **Adaptability**: As the legal landscape changes, being comfortable with technology ensures you can adapt to new tools and practices.

Developing the Necessary Skills

Legal Technology Skills

1. **Automation**: Learn how to use tools that automate routine tasks, such as document review and contract analysis.

2. **Data Analytics**: Understand how to analyze data to make informed decisions and provide better legal advice.
3. **Artificial Intelligence**: Gain familiarity with AI tools that can assist with legal research, drafting, and predictive analytics.

Example: An attorney uses an AI-driven contract analysis tool to identify potential risks and compliance issues in a client's contract, significantly reducing review time.

Business and Management Skills

1. **Project Management**: Learn how to manage legal projects efficiently, from planning to execution.
2. **Process Mapping**: Understand how to visualize and improve legal processes to increase efficiency and reduce costs.
3. **Business Analysis**: Develop the ability to analyze current practices and identify opportunities for improvement.

Example: A legal operations manager uses process mapping to streamline the firm's client intake process, reducing the time from initial contact to engagement.

Soft Skills

1. **Communication**: Develop strong communication skills to effectively collaborate with clients and colleagues.
2. **Networking**: Build a professional network to stay informed about industry trends and opportunities.
3. **Adaptability**: Be open to change and willing to learn new technologies and methodologies.

Example: A lawyer attends legal tech conferences and networking events to connect with other professionals and stay updated on the latest industry developments.

Cultivating a Digital Mindset

Embracing Change

Being open to new technologies and practices is crucial. This means actively seeking out new tools, learning how they work, and integrating them into your practice.

Example: A law firm adopts a cloud-based document management system to improve collaboration and accessibility for remote work.

Continuous Learning

Stay updated on the latest technological advancements and continuously seek to improve your skills. This can involve taking courses, attending webinars, and participating in professional development programs.

Example: A lawyer enrolls in an online course on blockchain technology and its applications in law, enhancing their ability to advise clients on cryptocurrency and smart contracts.

Leveraging Technology

Identify and implement technologies that can improve your practice. This includes using AI for legal research, automation tools for document review, and data analytics for case management.

Example: A legal team uses a predictive analytics tool to assess the likely outcome of litigation cases, allowing them to provide data-driven advice to clients.

Practical Steps to Becoming a Digital Legal Professional

Step 1: Assess Your Current Skills and Knowledge

Evaluate your current skill set and identify areas where you need to improve. This includes both legal and technological skills.

Example: A lawyer realizes they need to improve their data analysis skills and enrolls in a data analytics course to build this competency.

Step 2: Develop a Learning Plan

Create a plan for acquiring the necessary skills and knowledge. This should include specific goals, timelines, and resources for learning.

Example: A legal professional sets a goal to become proficient in legal project management within six months, using online courses and workshops to achieve this.

Step 3: Implement Digital Tools

Start using digital tools in your daily practice. Begin with tools that are easy to integrate and gradually adopt more advanced technologies.

Example: A law firm starts by implementing a client relationship management (CRM) system to better manage client interactions and then moves on to more complex tools like AI-powered legal research platforms.

Step 4: Network and Collaborate

Build a network of professionals in the legal tech field. Attend conferences, join online forums, and collaborate with colleagues to stay informed and share knowledge.

Example: A lawyer joins a local legal tech meetup group and attends monthly meetings to discuss the latest trends and tools in the industry.

Step 5: Continuously Evaluate and Improve

Regularly assess the effectiveness of the technologies and practices you have adopted. Seek feedback from colleagues and clients and make adjustments as needed.

Example: A legal operations manager conducts quarterly reviews of the firm's technology usage, gathering feedback from staff to identify areas for improvement and implement necessary changes.

Practical Examples

Example 1: Transitioning to a Digital Practice

Scenario: A solo practitioner wants to modernize their practice by adopting digital tools.

Actions: The lawyer starts by digitizing client files using a cloud-based document management system, adopts e-signature software for contracts, and begins using AI-powered legal research tools.

Outcome: The lawyer reduces administrative overhead, improves client communication, and provides faster, more accurate legal advice.

Example 2: Enhancing Efficiency with Automation

Scenario: A mid-sized law firm struggles with the time-consuming process of document review.

Actions: The firm implements an AI-powered document review tool that automatically identifies relevant information and flags potential issues.

Outcome: The document review process becomes significantly faster and more accurate, allowing lawyers to focus on strategic tasks.

Example 3: Leveraging Data Analytics for Better Decision Making

Scenario: A corporate legal department wants to improve its decision-making process.

Actions: The department adopts data analytics tools to analyze past case outcomes, track key performance indicators, and forecast litigation risks.

Outcome: The legal team can make more informed decisions, reducing legal risks and improving overall efficiency.

Conclusion

Becoming a digital legal professional involves developing a diverse set of skills, embracing a digital mindset, and leveraging technology to enhance your practice. By following the steps outlined in this chapter and continuously striving for improvement, you can position yourself for success in the rapidly evolving legal landscape.

USING DESIGN THINKING TO TRANSFORM YOUR LEGAL SERVICES

Introduction

Design thinking is a human-centered approach to problem-solving that emphasizes empathy, creativity, and iteration. It is particularly useful in the legal field, where understanding and addressing client needs are paramount. This chapter will introduce you to the concept of design thinking, its relevance in legal tech, and how to apply it in your practice. By the end of this chapter, you will have a comprehensive understanding of design thinking and how to use it to enhance your legal services.

Understanding Design Thinking

What is Design Thinking?

Design thinking is a methodology used to solve complex problems by focusing on the needs and experiences of users. It involves five key stages: empathize, define, ideate, prototype, and test. This iterative process helps legal professionals develop innovative solutions that are both effective and user-centric.

Example: A legal firm uses design thinking to revamp its client intake process. By empathizing with clients, defining their pain points, brainstorming ideas, prototyping new approaches, and testing them, the firm improves client satisfaction and efficiency.

Key Principles of Design Thinking

1. **Empathy**: Understanding the user's needs, experiences, and emotions.
2. **Collaboration**: Working with interdisciplinary teams to generate diverse ideas.
3. **Iteration**: Continuously refining solutions based on feedback.
4. **Creativity**: Encouraging innovative thinking and exploring multiple solutions.
5. **User-Centricity**: Keeping the user at the center of the design process.

Applying Design Thinking in Legal Tech

Empathize

Empathy involves understanding the needs, desires, and challenges of your clients. This can be achieved through interviews, surveys, and direct observations.

Example: A lawyer conducts in-depth interviews with clients to understand their frustrations with the current contract review process. This helps identify specific pain points and areas for improvement.

Define

In the define stage, you articulate the core problem based on insights gained during the empathy stage. This involves creating a clear problem statement that guides the ideation process.

Example: Based on client interviews, a law firm defines the problem as "Clients find the contract review process slow and confusing, leading to delays and misunderstandings."

Ideate

The ideation stage involves brainstorming and generating a wide range of ideas to address the defined problem. Encourage creativity and think outside the box.

Example: The law firm gathers a team to brainstorm solutions, such as implementing a client portal for real-time updates, using plain language summaries, and automating routine tasks with AI.

Prototype

Prototyping involves creating simple, tangible versions of the proposed solutions. These prototypes can be physical models, digital mockups, or process simulations.

Example: The firm develops a prototype of a client portal that provides real-time updates and plain language summaries of contracts. They also create a simple AI tool to automate routine contract review tasks.

Test

Testing involves evaluating the prototypes with real users to gather feedback and identify improvements. This stage is iterative, meaning you refine the prototypes based on feedback and test again.

Example: The firm tests the client portal and AI tool with a small group of clients, gathering feedback on usability and effectiveness. Based on the feedback, they make necessary adjustments and retest.

Real-World Examples of Design Thinking in Legal Tech

Example 1: Improving Client Communication

Scenario: A law firm wants to improve communication with clients during the litigation process.

Actions: The firm uses design thinking to empathize with clients, identifying their need for timely updates and clear explanations. They define the problem as "Clients feel uninformed and anxious due to lack of updates and unclear communication." The firm ideates solutions such as a dedicated case manager, regular status updates via email, and an online portal for case information. They prototype an online portal and test it with a few clients.

Outcome: Clients report increased satisfaction and reduced anxiety, leading to better client retention and referrals.

Example 2: Streamlining Contract Management

Scenario: A corporate legal department struggles with managing a high volume of contracts efficiently.

Actions: The department empathizes with internal stakeholders, defining the problem as "The current contract management process is time-consuming and prone to errors." They ideate solutions like a centralized digital repository, automated contract creation tools, and integrated approval workflows. Prototypes are developed and tested with a subset of users.

Outcome: The new system reduces contract processing time by 50% and decreases errors, resulting in significant cost savings and improved stakeholder satisfaction.

Tools and Techniques for Design Thinking

Empathy Tools

- **Interviews**: Conducting one-on-one interviews to gather deep insights.
- **Surveys**: Using structured questionnaires to collect data from a larger audience.
- **Observation**: Observing users in their natural environment to understand their behaviors and challenges.

Ideation Tools

- **Brainstorming**: Generating a large number of ideas in a short period.
- **Mind Mapping**: Visualizing ideas and their connections to facilitate creative thinking.

- **SCAMPER**: A technique that involves asking questions about existing processes/products to generate new ideas (Substitute, Combine, Adapt, Modify, Put to another use, Eliminate, and Reverse).

Prototyping Tools

- **Mockups**: Creating visual representations of the solution.
- **Wireframes**: Developing basic layouts for digital solutions.
- **Storyboards**: Illustrating the user journey through a series of sketches.

Testing Tools

- **User Testing**: Involving real users to test the prototypes and provide feedback.
- **A/B Testing**: Comparing two versions of a solution to determine which performs better.
- **Feedback Surveys**: Collecting structured feedback from users to identify areas for improvement.

Benefits of Design Thinking in Legal Tech

1. **Enhanced Client Satisfaction**: Solutions designed with user needs in mind lead to higher client satisfaction.
2. **Improved Efficiency**: Innovative processes and tools can streamline legal workflows, reducing time and costs.
3. **Increased Innovation**: Encouraging creative thinking leads to more innovative and effective solutions.
4. **Better Team Collaboration**: Design thinking promotes interdisciplinary collaboration, leading to more holistic solutions.

Conclusion

Design thinking is a powerful methodology that can transform legal practice by making it more user-centric, innovative, and efficient. By empathizing with clients, defining clear problems, ideating creative solutions, prototyping, and testing, legal professionals can develop solutions that truly meet client needs. Embracing design thinking not only enhances client satisfaction but also drives innovation and efficiency within legal organizations.

MASTERING LEGAL PROJECT MANAGEMENT (LPM): A COMPREHENSIVE GUIDE

Introduction

Legal Project Management (LPM) refers to the systematic approach to planning, executing, and completing legal projects with the goal of delivering high-quality legal services efficiently and cost-effectively. By integrating project management principles into legal practice, LPM helps legal professionals manage complex cases, control costs, and meet client expectations. This chapter will provide a comprehensive guide to LPM, complete with practical examples to illustrate key concepts and methodologies.

Understanding Legal Project Management

Definition

Legal Project Management (LPM) involves applying project management principles to legal projects. This includes planning, organizing, directing, and controlling resources to achieve specific goals within a defined timeframe and budget.

Example: A law firm uses LPM to manage a large-scale litigation case, ensuring all tasks are completed on time, within budget, and to the client's satisfaction.

Key Concepts

1. **Project Scope**: Clearly defining the objectives, deliverables, and boundaries of the project.
2. **Time Management**: Creating a timeline for project tasks and milestones.
3. **Cost Management**: Budgeting and controlling project costs.
4. **Quality Management**: Ensuring that the project meets the required standards.
5. **Resource Management**: Allocating and managing resources effectively.
6. **Risk Management**: Identifying and mitigating potential risks.
7. **Communication Management**: Facilitating effective communication among stakeholders.

The Legal Project Management Process

1. Initiation

The initiation phase involves defining the project scope, goals, and objectives. It includes conducting a risk assessment and obtaining approval to proceed.

Example: A legal team begins a new M&A project by defining the scope, identifying key stakeholders, and assessing potential risks.

2. Planning

In the planning phase, the project timeline is created, resources are allocated, and detailed plans for each task are developed. This phase also includes budgeting and creating a communication plan.

Example: The legal team creates a detailed project plan for the M&A project, including timelines, resource allocation, and a communication strategy.

3. Execution

During the execution phase, the project plan is put into action. Tasks are completed, progress is monitored, and adjustments are made as needed to stay on track.

Example: The legal team executes the M&A project plan, coordinating due diligence, drafting documents, and negotiating terms.

4. Monitoring and Controlling

This phase involves regular progress meetings, monitoring performance, and making necessary adjustments to ensure the project stays on track. It also includes problem-solving and risk management.

Example: The legal team holds weekly progress meetings to review the status of the M&A project, address any issues, and adjust the plan as needed.

5. Closing

The closing phase includes completing all project tasks, obtaining client approval, and conducting a post-project review to identify lessons learned and areas for improvement.

Example: After completing the M&A deal, the legal team conducts a post-project review to evaluate the process and identify improvements for future projects.

Project Management Methodologies

Waterfall

The Waterfall methodology is a linear, sequential approach where each phase is completed before moving on to the next. It is suitable for projects with well-defined requirements and limited changes.

Example: A legal team uses the Waterfall methodology for a straightforward contract review project, completing each phase sequentially.

Agile

Agile project management is an iterative and flexible approach that emphasizes continuous improvement and rapid delivery. It involves regular collaboration and feedback, making it ideal for projects with evolving requirements.

Example: A legal tech firm uses Agile methodology to develop a new software tool, working in short sprints and incorporating client feedback throughout the process.

Tools and Techniques for Legal Project Management

Risk Assessment

Conducting a risk assessment involves identifying potential risks, assessing their impact and likelihood, and developing mitigation strategies.

Example: A legal team uses a risk heat map to prioritize potential risks in a large litigation case, allowing them to allocate resources effectively.

Project Charter

A project charter outlines the project's scope, objectives, stakeholders, and execution plan. It serves as a reference document throughout the project.

Example: The legal team creates a project charter for an M&A project, detailing the scope, goals, stakeholders, and execution plan.

Gantt Chart

A Gantt chart provides a visual representation of the project schedule, showing the start and end dates of tasks, their duration, dependencies, and resource allocation.

Example: The legal team uses a Gantt chart to manage the timeline and tasks for a complex litigation case, ensuring all activities are completed on schedule.

Work Breakdown Structure (WBS)

A WBS is a hierarchical decomposition of the project into smaller, manageable components, typically broken down into tasks, subtasks, and work packages.

Example: The legal team creates a WBS for a contract management project, organizing tasks into clear, manageable components.

RACI Diagram

A RACI diagram is a matrix used to assign roles and responsibilities for tasks and decisions, with RACI standing for Responsible, Accountable, Consulted, and Informed.

Example: The legal team develops a RACI diagram for a compliance project, clarifying who is responsible for each task and who needs to be consulted or informed.

Communication Plan

A communication plan outlines how information will be shared among stakeholders and team members, including methods, frequency, and purpose.

Example: The legal team creates a communication plan for a regulatory compliance project, ensuring all stakeholders are kept informed throughout the project.

Project Estimating

Project estimating involves determining the resources, time, and costs needed to complete the project. Accurate estimates are crucial for budgeting and scheduling.

Example: The legal team uses historical data and expert judgment to estimate the time and cost required for a complex litigation case.

Project Review

A project review assesses the project's performance, identifies areas for improvement, and documents lessons learned. It is typically conducted at key milestones and at the end of the project.

Example: The legal team conducts a project review after completing an M&A deal, evaluating the process and identifying improvements for future projects.

Practical Examples of Legal Project Management

Example 1: Managing a Large Litigation Case

Scenario: A law firm is handling a large litigation case involving multiple parties and extensive documentation.

Actions: The firm uses LPM principles to define the project scope, create a detailed project plan, allocate resources, and establish a communication plan. They use a Gantt chart to manage the timeline and hold regular progress meetings.

Outcome: The litigation case is managed efficiently, with tasks completed on time and within budget, leading to a successful outcome for the client.

Example 2: Streamlining Contract Management

Scenario: A corporate legal department needs to streamline its contract management process.

Actions: The department uses LPM to create a project charter, develop a work breakdown structure, and implement an AI-powered contract analysis tool. They also establish a RACI diagram to clarify roles and responsibilities.

Outcome: The contract management process becomes more efficient, reducing review time and errors, and improving overall productivity.

Example 3: Developing a Legal Tech Solution

Scenario: A legal tech firm is developing a new software tool for document automation.

Actions: The firm adopts Agile methodology, working in short sprints and incorporating client feedback. They use a project charter, Gantt chart, and communication plan to manage the project.

Outcome: The software tool is developed iteratively, with continuous improvement based on user feedback, resulting in a high-quality product that meets client needs.

Conclusion

Legal Project Management is a critical discipline that helps legal professionals manage complex projects efficiently and effectively. By applying project management principles and using the right tools and techniques, legal teams can deliver high-quality services, control costs, and meet client expectations. Embracing LPM can lead to improved efficiency, better client satisfaction, and a competitive advantage in the legal industry.

UNDERSTANDING HOW LEGAL HACKATHONS ARE TRANSFORMING THE LEGAL INDUSTRY

Introduction

Legal hackathons are dynamic, collaborative events where legal professionals, developers, designers, and other stakeholders come together to create innovative solutions to pressing legal challenges. These events blend creativity, technology, and legal expertise, offering a unique platform for rapid prototyping and problem-solving. This chapter will explore the concept of legal hackathons, their benefits, and how to participate effectively. By the end of this chapter, you will have a comprehensive understanding of legal hackathons and how they can drive innovation in the legal field.

Understanding Legal Hackathons

What is a Legal Hackathon?

A legal hackathon is a collaborative event, typically lasting 24 to 48 hours, where participants work in teams to develop technology-driven solutions for legal problems. The term "hackathon" is derived from "hack," meaning to quickly put together, and "marathon," signifying the endurance required to work intensively over a short period.

Example: A legal hackathon might focus on developing an AI tool to streamline document review processes, bringing together lawyers, developers, and designers to brainstorm, build, and test their solution.

Key Components of a Legal Hackathon

1. **Workspace**: A conducive environment equipped with necessary resources such as laptops, reliable internet, and workstations.
2. **Teams**: Diverse groups of participants with complementary skills, including legal experts, developers, designers, and business strategists.
3. **Challenges**: Specific legal problems or themes that participants aim to address through their solutions.
4. **Mentors**: Experienced professionals who provide guidance, feedback, and support throughout the hackathon.
5. **Pitching**: The final presentation where teams showcase their solutions to a panel of judges or an audience.

Benefits of Legal Hackathons

Hands-On Experience

Legal hackathons provide practical, hands-on experience in applying technology to solve legal issues. Participants learn by doing, gaining insights into the tech industry and how it intersects with legal practice.

Example: A law student participating in a hackathon learns to use coding tools and collaborates with developers, enhancing their understanding of legal tech applications.

Innovation and Creativity

Hackathons foster a culture of innovation, encouraging participants to think creatively and develop out-of-the-box solutions to complex problems.

Example: A team develops a blockchain-based platform for secure and transparent property transactions, addressing issues of fraud and inefficiency in real estate law.

Networking Opportunities

These events offer excellent networking opportunities, allowing participants to connect with like-minded professionals, potential collaborators, and industry experts.

Example: A lawyer meets a tech entrepreneur at a hackathon and later collaborates with them to launch a legal tech startup.

Skill Development

Participants enhance their technical, legal, and project management skills, gaining a competitive edge in their careers.

Example: A legal professional learns project management techniques and agile methodologies, which they later apply to their practice.

Prototyping and Testing

Hackathons provide a platform for rapid prototyping and testing of ideas, allowing teams to validate their concepts quickly.

Example: A team develops a prototype of an AI tool for legal research, tests it during the hackathon, and receives valuable feedback for further development.

How to Participate in a Legal Hackathon

Finding a Hackathon

Look for hackathons hosted by law schools, legal tech companies, bar associations, or industry groups. Many events are advertised online through websites, social media, and professional networks.

Example: LegalTech Fest, an annual event featuring various legal tech hackathons and workshops.

Preparing for the Hackathon

1. **Form a Team**: Assemble a diverse team with complementary skills. If you don't have a team, many hackathons allow individual registration and help form teams on-site.
2. **Research the Theme**: Understand the theme or problem statement of the hackathon and conduct preliminary research to gather insights.
3. **Gather Resources**: Bring necessary tools and resources, such as laptops, chargers, and any specific software or materials you might need.

Example: A team preparing for a hackathon focused on access to justice issues researches existing solutions and gathers data on underserved communities.

During the Hackathon

1. **Define the Problem**: Clearly articulate the problem you are addressing and ensure everyone on the team understands it.
2. **Ideate Solutions**: Brainstorm multiple ideas and evaluate their feasibility. Encourage creative thinking and explore various approaches.
3. **Prototype Rapidly**: Develop a minimum viable product (MVP) or prototype quickly. Focus on core functionalities that demonstrate your concept.
4. **Test and Iterate**: Test your prototype, gather feedback from mentors and peers, and iterate to improve your solution.
5. **Prepare Your Pitch**: Create a compelling presentation that explains the problem, your solution, and its impact. Practice your pitch to ensure clarity and confidence.

Example: A team working on an online dispute resolution platform quickly develops a basic prototype, tests it with mentors, and refines the user interface based on feedback.

After the Hackathon

1. **Gather Feedback**: Collect feedback from judges, mentors, and other participants to understand the strengths and weaknesses of your solution.
2. **Follow Up**: Stay in touch with new contacts and explore potential collaborations or opportunities that arose during the event.
3. **Refine and Develop**: Continue working on your solution, incorporating feedback and further developing your prototype into a fully functional product.

Example: A team receives positive feedback on their legal chatbot prototype and decides to continue development, eventually launching it as a commercial product.

Case Study: Tech for Justice Legal Hackathon

Background

The Tech for Justice Legal Hackathon aimed to address issues such as court closures, legal aid cuts, and unequal access to legal services. The goal was to create transparent, fair, efficient, and accessible justice systems.

Process

1. **Problem Definition**: Participants identified key challenges faced by citizens due to court closures and legal aid cuts.
2. **Team Formation**: Teams were formed with a mix of legal professionals, developers, and designers.
3. **Ideation and Prototyping**: Teams brainstormed solutions and developed prototypes over a 48-hour period.
4. **Testing and Feedback**: Prototypes were tested, and feedback was gathered from mentors and judges.
5. **Pitching**: Teams presented their solutions to a panel of judges.

Outcome

One of the top solutions was an AI-powered platform that provided free legal information and advice to citizens, helping them navigate the legal system more effectively. The solution was well-received and recognized for its potential to improve access to justice.

Conclusion

Legal hackathons are powerful platforms for innovation, collaboration, and skill development. By participating in a legal hackathon, you can gain hands-on experience, network with professionals, and contribute to solving pressing legal challenges. Whether you are a seasoned lawyer or a law student, hackathons offer valuable opportunities to enhance your skills, explore new ideas, and make a meaningful impact in the legal field.

LEGAL STARTUPS: SHAPING THE FUTURE OF THE LEGAL INDUSTRY

Introduction

Legal startups have emerged as significant disruptors in the legal industry, leveraging technology and innovative business models to challenge traditional practices and improve access to legal services. These startups offer new solutions that enhance efficiency, reduce costs, and make legal services more accessible to a broader audience. This chapter will explore the landscape of legal startups, their impact on the legal industry, and provide practical examples to illustrate their influence.

Understanding Legal Startups

What is a Legal Startup?

A legal startup is a company that uses technology to provide innovative legal services or solutions. These startups often focus on addressing specific pain points within the legal industry, such as inefficiency, high costs, and limited access to legal services.

Example: LegalZoom, founded in 2001, provides online legal services, making it easier and more affordable for individuals and small businesses to access legal assistance.

Key Characteristics of Legal Startups

1. **Innovation**: Legal startups leverage cutting-edge technology to create new solutions for legal problems.
2. **Efficiency**: They focus on streamlining processes and reducing the time and cost associated with legal services.
3. **Accessibility**: By offering affordable and user-friendly solutions, legal startups make legal services more accessible to a wider audience.
4. **Scalability**: These startups design their solutions to be easily scalable, allowing them to serve a growing number of clients without a proportional increase in costs.

The Impact of Legal Startups on the Legal Industry

Disruption of Traditional Models

Legal startups have disrupted traditional law firm models by introducing alternative fee arrangements and innovative service delivery methods. Traditional law firms often operate on a time-based billing model, which can be inefficient and expensive for clients. In contrast, legal startups offer alternative pricing models such as flat fees, subscription-based services, and value-based pricing.

Example: Rocket Lawyer offers legal services on a subscription basis, providing clients with affordable access to legal documents, advice, and attorney consultations.

Enhanced Collaboration and Communication

Legal startups emphasize seamless communication and collaboration within firms and with clients. This approach leads to better outcomes for clients and a more efficient work environment.

Example: Clio, a legal practice management software, enhances collaboration by providing a centralized platform for case management, document sharing, and client communication.

Integration of Non-Lawyers

Legal startups have expanded the scope of the legal industry by incorporating non-lawyers, such as technology experts and business strategists, into their operations. This interdisciplinary approach brings fresh perspectives and innovative solutions to the delivery of legal services.

Example: Juro, a legal tech startup, integrates software developers, UX designers, and legal experts to create a platform that streamlines contract management and improves user experience.

Global Reach and Investment

The legal tech market has seen significant growth globally, with notable activity in North America, Europe, and Asia. Legal startups have attracted substantial investment, enabling them to develop advanced solutions and expand their market reach.

Example: DocuSign, a legal tech company specializing in electronic signatures, has raised over $1 billion in funding and operates in multiple countries, transforming how businesses handle agreements.

Practical Examples of Legal Startups

Example 1: LegalZoom

Scenario: LegalZoom, founded in 2001, aims to make legal services accessible and affordable for individuals and small businesses.

Actions: The company offers a range of online legal services, including document preparation, business formation, and legal advice. Clients can access these services through a user-friendly platform without the need for in-person consultations.

Outcome: LegalZoom has democratized access to legal services, serving millions of customers and becoming a market leader in online legal solutions.

Example 2: Clio

Scenario: Clio, founded in 2008, provides cloud-based legal practice management software for law firms.

Actions: The software offers features such as case management, time tracking, billing, and client communication. Clio integrates with various other tools, enhancing its functionality and user experience.

Outcome: Clio has improved the efficiency of legal practices by centralizing case management and facilitating better collaboration among legal teams. It is now used by thousands of law firms worldwide.

Example 3: Juro

Scenario: Juro, founded in 2016, focuses on simplifying contract management for businesses.

Actions: Juro offers a platform that automates contract creation, negotiation, and management. The platform integrates with other business tools and uses AI to streamline the contract workflow.

Outcome: Juro has significantly reduced the time and complexity associated with contract management, helping businesses manage their contracts more efficiently and effectively.

Example 4: Presolv360

Scenario: Presolv360, founded in 2017, aims to streamline the legal discovery process in India.

Actions: The platform provides tools for document management, case tracking, and automated workflows. It also offers an AI-powered discovery engine that helps legal teams quickly identify relevant documents.

Outcome: Presolv360 has enhanced the efficiency of the legal discovery process, reducing the time and cost involved in managing legal cases for organizations in India.

How to Start a Legal Tech Startup

Identify a Problem

Successful legal startups begin by identifying a specific problem or pain point within the legal industry. Conduct thorough research to understand the needs of your target market and the gaps in existing services.

Example: A legal tech entrepreneur identifies the need for more efficient and affordable access to legal advice for small businesses.

Develop a Solution

Create a solution that addresses the identified problem. Focus on innovation, efficiency, and user experience. Develop a minimum viable product (MVP) to test your concept and gather feedback.

Example: The entrepreneur develops a platform that connects small businesses with experienced lawyers for affordable, on-demand legal advice.

Build a Team

Assemble a team with diverse skills, including legal expertise, technology development, business strategy, and marketing. A strong team is crucial for the success of your startup.

Example: The entrepreneur recruits a team of lawyers, software developers, and business strategists to build and launch the platform.

Secure Funding

Explore various funding options such as angel investors, venture capital, grants, and crowdfunding. Prepare a compelling pitch deck to attract potential investors.

Example: The startup secures seed funding from an angel investor to develop and launch the platform.

Launch and Iterate

Launch your MVP and gather feedback from early users. Use this feedback to refine and improve your solution. Continuously iterate and adapt to meet the evolving needs of your target market.

Example: The startup launches the platform, gathers user feedback, and makes necessary improvements to enhance functionality and user experience.

Conclusion

Legal startups are transforming the legal industry by introducing innovative solutions that enhance efficiency, reduce costs, and improve access to legal services. By understanding the landscape of legal startups, their impact, and how to successfully launch a legal tech startup, legal professionals can embrace the opportunities created by this dynamic and rapidly evolving sector.

GENERATIVE AI (GAI) IN LAW: APPLICATIONS, BENEFITS, AND FUTURE TRENDS

Introduction

The legal industry is on the cusp of a transformative era driven by Generative AI (GAI). Unlike traditional AI, which excels at pattern recognition, GAI possesses the remarkable ability to create entirely new content, including legal documents, contracts, and even legal arguments. This capability has the potential to disrupt the legal landscape fundamentally, altering how legal services are delivered and consumed. This chapter explores the applications, benefits, challenges, and future of GAI in legal services, with practical examples to illustrate its impact.

The Potential of Generative AI in Legal Services

Generative AI has the potential to automate a significant portion of legal tasks, freeing up lawyers from mundane, repetitive work and allowing them to focus on more complex, strategic matters. A recent study by Goldman Sachs estimates that GAI can automate up to 44% of legal tasks, a significantly higher percentage than in any other profession. Here are some specific applications of GAI in legal services:

Textual Content Generation

GAI can draft contracts, legal memoranda, policies, and advisory communications, reducing the time and effort required for these tasks.

Example: A law firm uses GAI to draft standard contracts, allowing lawyers to focus on customizing and reviewing complex clauses rather than starting from scratch.

Classification

GAI can categorize legal documents for due diligence or populate knowledge management databases, improving organization and accessibility.

Example: During a due diligence process, GAI automatically categorizes thousands of documents, streamlining the review process and ensuring that relevant documents are easily accessible.

Summarization

GAI can condense complex legal documents and research findings, making them easier to understand and analyze.

Example: A lawyer receives a 200-page case file and uses GAI to generate a concise summary, highlighting the key points and legal issues, saving hours of manual review.

Transformation

GAI can simplify legal language for better client comprehension, making legal documents more accessible to non-experts.

Example: A legal aid organization uses GAI to rewrite complex legal documents in plain language, helping clients understand their rights and obligations more clearly.

Question and Answer (Q&A)

GAI can answer legal inquiries from clients or internal stakeholders, providing quick and accurate information.

Example: A law firm implements a GAI-powered chatbot to answer common client questions about legal procedures, freeing up lawyers to handle more complex inquiries.

Extraction

GAI can extract critical information from legal documents for due diligence or contract review, improving accuracy and efficiency.

Example: During a merger, GAI extracts key terms and conditions from hundreds of contracts, enabling the legal team to identify potential issues quickly.

Reasoning

GAI can analyze legal issues and predict potential outcomes, providing valuable insights for decision-making.

Example: A litigation team uses GAI to analyze past case outcomes and predict the likelihood of success in a new case, helping them develop a more effective strategy.

Benefits and Opportunities

The adoption of GAI in legal services presents a multitude of benefits and opportunities:

Increased Productivity

Lawyers can accomplish more in less time by delegating routine tasks to GAI, allowing them to focus on higher-value work.

Example: A law firm reports a 30% increase in productivity after implementing GAI tools for document drafting and review.

Enhanced Accuracy

GAI can analyze vast amounts of legal data to ensure consistency and minimize errors, improving the quality of legal services.

Example: A legal team uses GAI to check contracts for inconsistencies, reducing the error rate by 25%.

Reduced Costs

Automating tasks and streamlining workflows can significantly reduce the cost of legal services, making them more affordable.

Example: A small business uses a GAI-powered platform to draft and review contracts, saving thousands of dollars in legal fees.

Improved Access to Justice

GAI-powered legal tools can make legal services more affordable and accessible to a wider audience, bridging the justice gap.

Example: A nonprofit organization uses GAI to provide free legal advice to low-income individuals, helping them navigate the legal system.

Democratization of Legal Expertise

GAI can empower individuals with the ability to handle basic legal matters without needing a lawyer, democratizing access to legal expertise.

Example: An entrepreneur uses a GAI tool to draft and file incorporation documents, eliminating the need for costly legal assistance.

Challenges and Considerations

While GAI holds immense promise for the legal field, there are also challenges and considerations to address:

Accuracy and Reliability

GAI models are still under development, and their outputs require careful validation by human experts to ensure accuracy and reliability.

Example: A law firm using GAI for contract review assigns junior lawyers to verify the AI's output, ensuring that no critical issues are overlooked.

Data Privacy and Security

Legal professionals must ensure that the data used to train GAI models is secure and compliant with data privacy regulations.

Example: A legal tech company implements robust encryption and data anonymization techniques to protect client information used in GAI training.

Bias and Fairness

GAI models can perpetuate biases present in the data they are trained on. Careful attention is needed to mitigate bias in legal applications.

Example: A legal research firm conducts regular audits of its GAI models to identify and address any biases, ensuring fair and equitable outcomes.

Impact on Legal Jobs

Automation through GAI may lead to job displacement in the legal sector. However, it is also likely to create new opportunities for lawyers with specialized skills in GAI and legal technology.

Example: A paralegal retrains as a legal tech specialist, managing the implementation and oversight of GAI tools within their firm.

The Path Forward

The legal industry is rapidly embracing GAI, and early adopters are already reaping the benefits. Here are some steps corporate legal departments can take to leverage GAI:

Identify Use Cases

Analyze current workflows and identify tasks that are well-suited for GAI automation. Focus on repetitive, time-consuming tasks that can benefit from increased efficiency.

Example: A legal department identifies document review, contract drafting, and legal research as key areas for GAI implementation.

Evaluate GAI Solutions

Explore the different GAI solutions available, considering factors like specialization, accuracy, and ease of use. Conduct pilot tests to evaluate their effectiveness.

Example: A law firm conducts a pilot program with three different GAI vendors, assessing their performance and selecting the best fit for their needs.

Develop a Pilot Program

Start with a small-scale GAI pilot program to test its effectiveness and identify potential challenges. Use the pilot to gather data and refine your implementation strategy.

Example: A corporate legal department launches a pilot program to use GAI for contract review, monitoring its impact on efficiency and accuracy.

Invest in Training

Train lawyers and staff on how to use GAI effectively and interpret its outputs. Continuous learning is essential to keep pace with technological advancements.

Example: A law firm offers regular training sessions on GAI tools, ensuring that all team members are proficient and comfortable using the technology.

Conclusion

Generative AI is poised to revolutionize the legal industry. By understanding its potential, challenges, and implementation strategies, legal professionals can harness this transformative technology to deliver better, faster, and more affordable legal services. The future of legal services is intelligent, automated, and accessible, and Generative AI is paving the way for this exciting new era.

HOW GENERATIVE AI IS REVOLUTIONIZING THE LEGAL LANDSCAPE

Introduction

Generative AI (GAI) is revolutionizing the legal industry by creating entirely new content such as contracts, legal documents, and even arguments. Unlike traditional AI, which primarily analyzes patterns, GAI can draft, summarize, and generate content, fundamentally transforming legal workflows. This chapter will explore the workings of GAI, its benefits, challenges, and provide practical examples to illustrate its transformative impact on the legal landscape.

What is Generative AI and How Does it Work in Law?

Generative AI is a type of artificial intelligence that can create new content based on the data it has been trained on. In the legal field, GAI can draft contracts, summarize complex documents, and even generate legal arguments. This capability can revolutionize legal workflows by automating repetitive tasks and allowing lawyers to focus on more strategic work.

Example: A law firm uses GAI to draft initial versions of contracts. The AI generates a first draft based on the firm's templates and past contracts, which the lawyers then review and customize as needed.

How GAI Works in Law

1. **Data Input**: GAI models are trained on vast amounts of legal data, including case law, statutes, contracts, and other legal documents.

2. **Content Generation**: Once trained, GAI can generate new content by predicting what comes next in a sequence based on the patterns it has learned.

3. **Human Oversight**: Lawyers review and refine the AI-generated content to ensure accuracy and compliance with legal standards.

Benefits and Opportunities

Generative AI offers numerous benefits and opportunities for the legal industry:

Increased Productivity

By automating routine tasks such as document generation and classification, GAI allows lawyers to focus on complex and strategic work, significantly boosting overall productivity.

Example: A legal department automates the generation of routine contracts using GAI, allowing its lawyers to dedicate more time to negotiation and strategic planning.

Enhanced Accuracy

GAI can analyze vast amounts of data to generate content with a high degree of accuracy, minimizing errors that may occur in manual drafting.

Example: A law firm uses GAI to review and correct contracts for consistency and accuracy, reducing the error rate in contract management.

Reduced Costs

Automation of legal tasks streamlines workflows and reduces the time and resources needed to complete them, making legal services more affordable.

Example: A startup uses GAI to automate its compliance documentation, reducing legal costs and ensuring timely compliance with regulations.

Improved Access to Justice

GAI-powered tools can make legal help more accessible to individuals and small businesses by providing affordable and efficient legal services.

Example: A non-profit organization uses GAI to offer free legal advice and document drafting services to low-income individuals, improving access to justice.

Democratization of Expertise

GAI enables individuals to handle basic legal matters themselves, with AI assistance, democratizing access to legal expertise.

Example: An entrepreneur uses a GAI-powered platform to draft and file incorporation documents, eliminating the need for expensive legal assistance.

Challenges and Considerations

While GAI offers significant benefits, there are also challenges and considerations to address:

Accuracy and Reliability

GAI models are still under development, and their outputs require careful validation by human experts to ensure accuracy and reliability.

Example: A law firm assigns junior lawyers to verify the output of GAI-generated documents, ensuring that all content meets legal standards and is free of errors.

Bias and Fairness

GAI can perpetuate biases present in the data it is trained on. It is crucial to implement measures to mitigate bias and ensure fairness in AI-generated content.

Example: A legal research firm conducts regular audits of its GAI models to identify and address any biases, ensuring that the AI outputs are fair and equitable.

Data Privacy and Security

Ensuring the security and privacy of data used to train GAI models is paramount, especially given the sensitive nature of legal information.

Example: A legal tech company uses advanced encryption and data anonymization techniques to protect client information during the training of GAI models.

Impact on Legal Jobs

Automation through GAI may lead to job displacement in the legal sector. However, it also creates new opportunities for lawyers with specialized skills in GAI and legal technology.

Example: A paralegal retrains as a legal tech specialist, managing the implementation and oversight of GAI tools within their firm.

Getting Started with Generative AI: A Roadmap for Your Practice

Identify Use Cases

Analyze your current workflows and identify tasks that are best suited for GAI automation. Focus on repetitive, time-consuming tasks that can benefit from increased efficiency.

Example: A corporate legal department identifies contract review, document drafting, and legal research as key areas for GAI implementation.

Evaluate Solutions

Explore various GAI solutions available in the market, considering factors such as specialization, accuracy, and ease of use. Conduct pilot tests to evaluate their effectiveness.

Example: A law firm conducts a pilot program with three different GAI vendors, assessing their performance and selecting the best fit for their needs.

Develop a Pilot Program

Start with a small-scale GAI pilot program to test its effectiveness and identify potential challenges. Use the pilot to gather data and refine your implementation strategy.

Example: A corporate legal department launches a pilot program to use GAI for contract review, monitoring its impact on efficiency and accuracy.

Invest in Training

Train lawyers and staff on how to use GAI effectively and interpret its outputs. Continuous learning is essential to keep pace with technological advancements.

Example: A law firm offers regular training sessions on GAI tools, ensuring that all team members are proficient and comfortable using the technology.

The Future of Generative AI in Law: A Glimpse Ahead

The future of legal services is intelligent and automated. We can expect even more sophisticated GAI applications such as legal reasoning, contract negotiation, and predictive analytics. Regulatory frameworks are evolving to address potential risks such as bias and data privacy. GAI will likely reshape legal service delivery models and the lawyer-client relationship.

Example: A law firm uses GAI to predict the outcomes of litigation cases based on historical data, helping clients make informed decisions about whether to settle or proceed to trial.

Conclusion

Generative AI is transforming the legal landscape by automating routine tasks, enhancing accuracy, and making legal services more accessible. By understanding GAI's potential and challenges, legal professionals can harness this transformative technology to deliver better, faster, and more affordable legal services. The future of legal services is intelligent, automated, and accessible, and Generative AI is paving the way for this exciting new era.

CONCLUSION

As we conclude our journey through **"Mastering Legal Tech and AI: Tools, Trends, Innovations, and Transformations That Lawyers, Law Students, and Professionals Must Know in Modern Law Practice and Justice,"** it's clear that we are standing at the precipice of a new era in the legal profession. The advancements in technology and artificial intelligence offer unprecedented opportunities to enhance efficiency, improve accuracy, and provide superior client service.

Throughout this book, we have explored the transformative power of legal technology and AI. From understanding the basics of blockchain and smart contracts to delving into the intricacies of AI-driven legal research and analytics, we have equipped you with the knowledge to navigate this dynamic landscape. We have also addressed the ethical considerations and professional implications, ensuring that you are prepared to implement these technologies responsibly and effectively.

Knowledge alone is not enough; action is the key to transformation. As you close this book, I urge you to take the insights and strategies you've gained and apply them to your practice. Start small, experiment with new tools, and gradually integrate more advanced technologies. By embracing a digital mindset and continually seeking to innovate, you will position yourself at the forefront of the legal profession.

The future of law is not just about keeping up with change; it's about leading it. Be proactive in seeking out new opportunities, and don't be afraid to challenge the status quo. Whether you're a seasoned lawyer looking to modernize your practice, a law student eager to enter the profession with a competitive edge, or a legal professional striving to stay relevant, you have the power to shape the future of law.

Final Thoughts

As we move forward, remember that the journey of mastering legal tech and AI is ongoing. Stay curious, stay informed, and stay committed to excellence. The tools and knowledge you've acquired from this book are just the beginning. Use them to innovate, to solve complex problems, and to deliver exceptional value to your clients.

Thank you for joining me on this journey. Now, it's time to take action. Embrace the future, lead with technology, and become a pioneer in the modern legal landscape.

CHECK OUT OTHER BOOKS

Go here to check out other related books that might interest you:

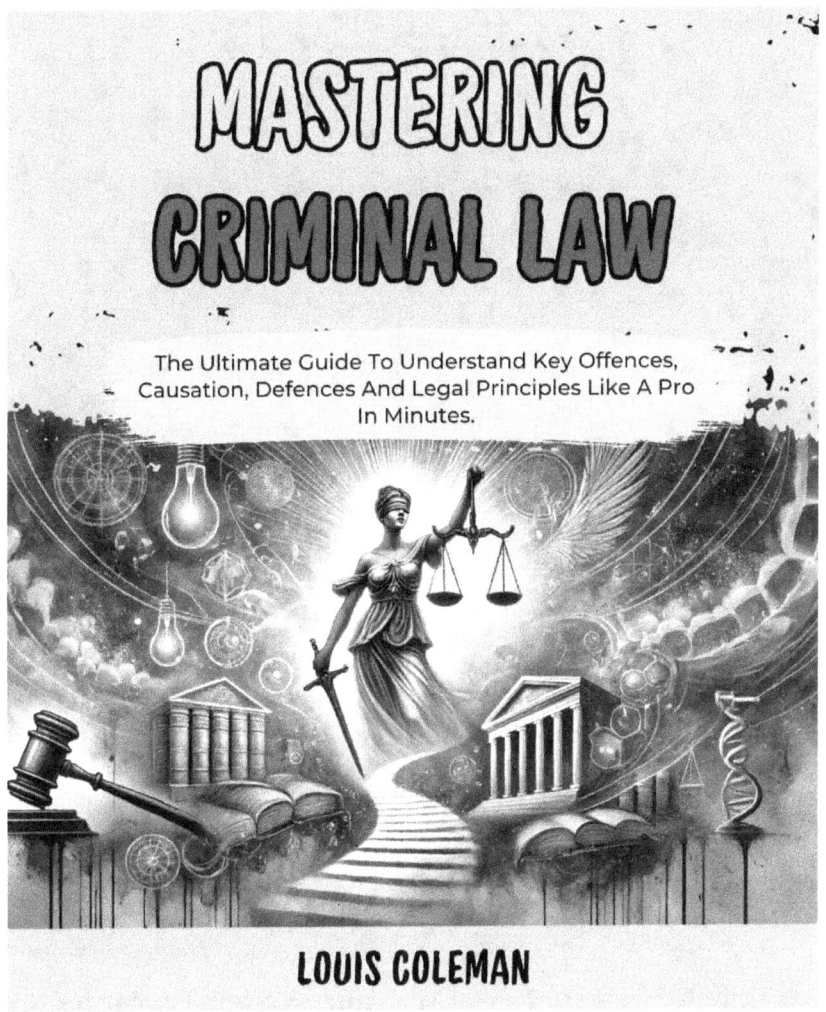

Mastering Criminal Law: The Ultimate Guide To Understand Key Offences, Causation, Defences And Legal Principles Like A Pro In Minutes.

https://www.amazon.com/dp/B0D4H97Y7B

Mastering Academic Legal Writing: A Step-By-Step Guide, Proven Techniques, Tips And Strategies For Crafting Powerful And Compelling Legal Documents Like A Pro In Minutes.

https://www.amazon.com/dp/B0D7J6FNTY

Mastering Business Writing: A Step-By-Step Guide, Proven Techniques, Tips & Strategies For Crafting Powerful And Compelling Business Letters, Reports, Proposals and Emails Like A Pro In Minutes.

https://www.amazon.com/dp/B0D7N1Y8VM

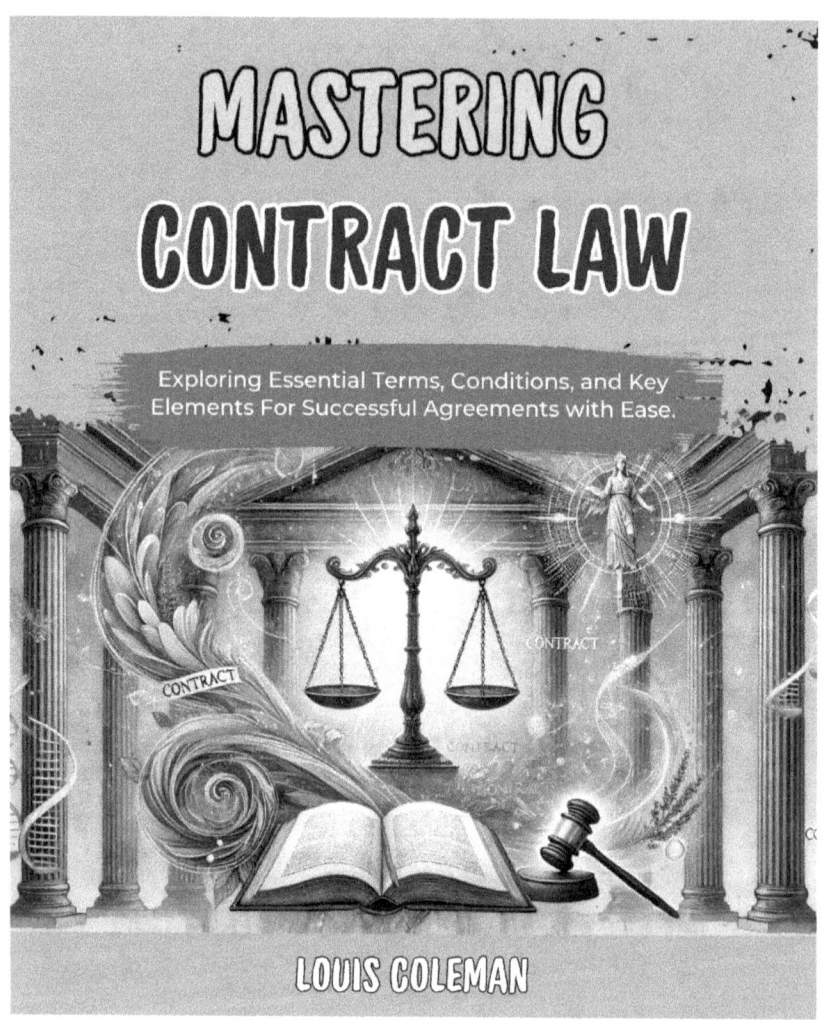

Mastering Contract Law: Exploring Essential Terms, Conditions, and Key Elements For Successful Agreements with Ease.

https://www.amazon.com/dp/B0D7Q6QRF5

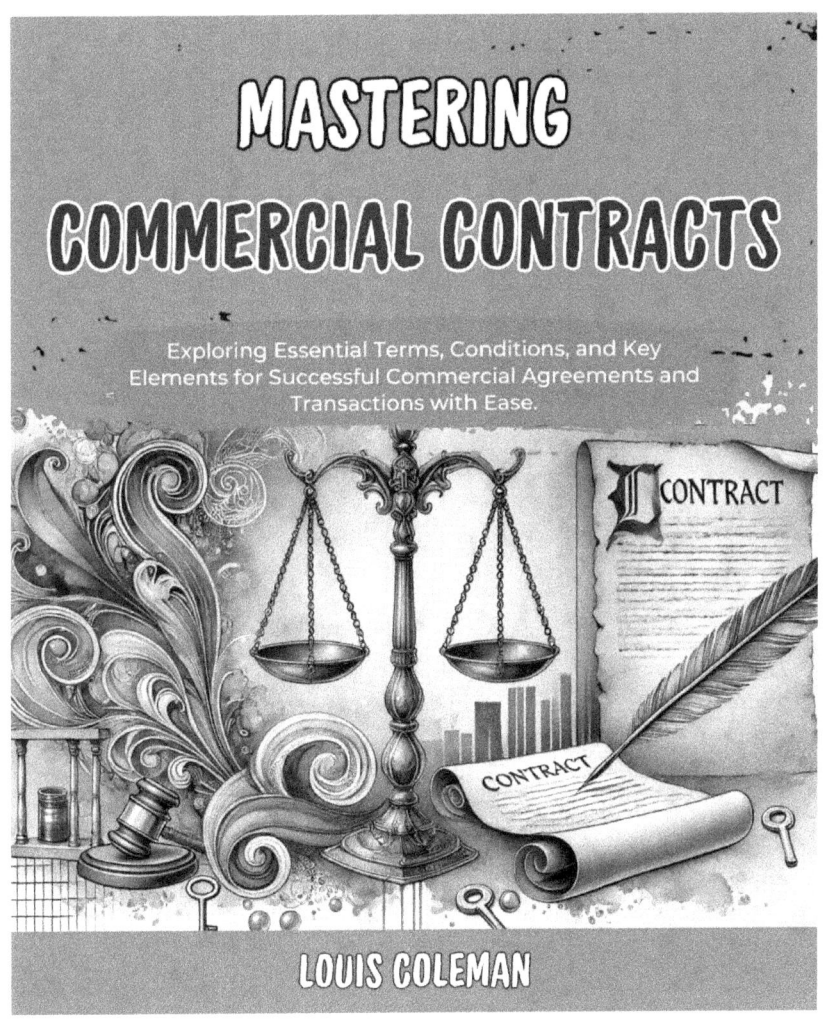

Mastering Commercial Contracts: Exploring Essential Terms, Conditions, and Key Elements For Successful Commercial Agreements and Transactions with Ease.

https://www.amazon.com/dp/B0D7TRSYLM

Mastering Commercial Law: Your Ultimate Guide to Understanding Key Business Structures and Terms Related To Sole Proprietorships, Partnerships, and Corporations Like A Pro In Minutes.

https://www.amazon.com/dp/B0D7W67S34

Kindle Publishing Guidelines: The Ultimate Guide, Tips, Tricks, Secrets On How To Generate A Huge Passive Income With Your Own Books Within A Short Period Of Time.

https://www.amazon.com/dp/B0CW1MJXDW

Cryptocurrency Investment Strategies: A Step By Step Guide, Tips, Tricks, Secrets And Strategies To Invest Successfully And Become A Millionaire In Cryptocurrency.

https://www.amazon.com/dp/B0D7611C9C

Design Like A Pro With Canva: The Step By Step Canva Guide To Create Professional Graphics And Transform Your Designs Instantly.

https://www.amazon.com/dp/B0D6FDQZKF

Canva Mastery For Beginners: The Complete Canva Expert Guide To Design Everything With Ease And Fast Like A Pro.

https://www.amazon.com/dp/B0D2VXN8KB

Crack Ielts Speaking Part 1: Proven Secrets, Tips and Strategies On How To Achieve An 8.0+ Band Score in Ielts Speaking Part 1 Easily.

https://www.amazon.com/dp/B0CYB14RFW

Crack Ielts Writing Task 2: Excellent Sample Answers By Topics, Tips and Strategies On How To Achieve An 8.0+ Band Score in Ielts Writing Task 2 Easily.

https://www.amazon.com/dp/B0CXJSNZSG

Ielts Speaking Part 1 By Topics: Over 200 Excellent Sample Answers By Topics You Must Know To Achieve An 8.0+ Band Score In Ielts Speaking Part 1 Easily.

https://www.amazon.com/dp/B0D2VWJHDR

Ielts Speaking Part 2 By Topics: Over 100 Excellent Sample Answers By Topics You Must Know To Achieve An 8.0+ Band Score In Ielts Speaking Part 2 Easily.

https://www.amazon.com/dp/B0D2S5ZDP6

Mastering IELTS Speaking: Achieve Band 8.0+ in Ielts Speaking with Proven Strategies, Excellent Sample Answers and Practice Exercises.

https://www.amazon.com/dp/B0CW6C9HK8

Mastering Ielts Writing: Achieve Band 8.0+ in Ielts Writing with Proven Strategies, Excellent Sample Answers and Practice Exercises.

https://www.amazon.com/dp/B0D4TD1NLC

Ielts Writing For Success: The Complete Guide To Achieve Band 8.0+ In Ielts Writing With Proven Strategies, Vocabulary & Excellent Sample Answers In 2 Weeks.

https://www.amazon.com/dp/B0D4W6JVRR

Mastering Ielts Reading: Achieve Band 8.0+ Easily in Ielts Reading with Proven Strategies, Tips, Tricks and Techniques.

https://www.amazon.com/dp/B0D2BJZBS8

www.ingramcontent.com/pod-product-compliance
Lightning Source LLC
Chambersburg PA
CBHW071827210526
45479CB00001B/26